# ADULT ONLY
# BLONDE
# JOKES

*Guaranteed to make you giggle!*

HB
HINKLER
BOOKS

Joke Compilation: Scribblers and Writers
Cover Design: Sam Grimmer
Illustrations: John Shakespeare
Editor: Jasmine Chan
Typesetting: Midland Typesetters, Maryborough, VIC, Australia

Adults Only Blonde Jokes
First Published in 2004 by Hinkler Books Pty Ltd
17–23 Redwood Drive
Dingley VIC 3172 Australia
www.hinklerbooks.com

First printed in 2004

ISBN: 1 7412 1657 5

Printed and bound in Australia

# INTRODUCTION

I t's a tough life being a blonde. Even the first joke in this book endeavours to fix that difficult situation.

The poor old blonde has copped it for being an air-head, vacuous, stupid, incapable of thought, having no sense at all and just being plain dumb.

*And that's just the blokes . . .*

Indeed, this blonde book has just as many jokes about blonde blokes (technically speaking who are 'blond' as distinct from 'blonde', but let's not get too grammatically picky), as it does about blonde girls.

It's gone on for 20 years now. And blonde jokes are still a great source of a good laugh.

Well, for the rest of us who are not blonde/blond, that is . . .

# THE BLONDE WAY

There was the blonde who was complaining to her friend about constantly being called a dumb blonde.

Her friend tells her, 'Go do something to prove them wrong! Why don't you learn all the world capitals or something?'

The blonde thinks this is a great idea and locks herself up for two weeks studying.

The next party she goes to, some guy is making dumb blonde comments to her.

She gets all indignant and claims, 'I'm not a dumb blonde. In fact, I can name all the world capitals!'

The guy doesn't believe her, so she dares him to test her.

He says, 'Okay, what's the capital of Monaco?'

The blonde tosses her hair in triumph and says, 'That's easy! It's M!'

A young blonde woman is distraught because she fears her husband is having an affair, so she goes to a gun shop and buys a handgun.

The next day she comes home to find her husband in bed with a beautiful redhead.

She grabs the gun and holds it to her own head.

The husband jumps out of bed, begging and pleading with her not to shoot herself. Hysterically the blonde responds to the husband, 'Shut up . . . you're next!'

There was a blonde driving through the country.

She just dyed her hair brown, because she was sick of being made fun of her hair colour.

She was really hungry so she stopped at a farmer's house and says, 'Hi! If I can guess how many sheep you have, can I have one?'

The farmer agreed.

So she quickly counted them and said, '91.'

The farmer looked around puzzled and said, 'Okay. Take one.'

When the blonde was walking back to her car the farmer asked, 'If I can guess your natural hair colour, can I have my dog back?'

Three blondes are stuck on a deserted island, when one of them finds a lamp on the beach.

She picks it up and gives it a little rub and a genie pops out. The genie looks at the three blondes and says, 'I normally give three wishes, but since there are three of you, I will grant each of you one wish.'

Well, the first one is tired of being on the island, so she wishes to go back home. Poof! She disappears.

The second one said she, too, is tired of the island and wishes to go home. Poof! She also disappears.

The genie then turns to the last blonde and asks her what her wish is.

'Gee,' she says, 'I'm awfully lonely here by myself. I wish my friends were still here.'

Derek drove his brand new Mercedes to his favourite bar and put it in the car park at the back. He went inside, where the bar was being looked after by Beverley, the blonde waitress.

As Derek walked into the bar, she happily greeted him. He bought a drink and went and sat at a table.

A few minutes later, Beverley came running up to him yelling, 'Derek! Derek! I was putting the trash out the back and just saw someone driving off with your new Mercedes!'

'Dear God! Did you try to stop him?'

'No,' she said, 'I did better than that! I got the licence plate number!'

Back in the old Wild West, there were two blonde cowpokes, Jeff and Dave.

One day, the two were enjoying a drink in the local saloon, when a man walked into the bar with an Indian's head under his arm.

The barman shakes his hand and said, 'I hate Indians; last week the bastards burnt my barn to the ground, assaulted my wife and killed my children.'

He then added, 'If any man brings me the head of an Indian, I'll give him $1000.'

The two blondes looked at each other and walked out of the bar to go hunting for an Indian.

They found one. Jeff threw a rock which hit the Indian right on the head.

The Indian fell off his horse, but landed 70 feet down a ravine.

The two blondes made their way down the ravine where Dave pulled out a knife ready to claim their trophy.

Jeff called urgently, 'Dave, take a look at this.'

Dave replied, 'Not now, I'm busy.'

Jeff tries again with more panic in his voice and says, 'I really think you should look at this.'

Dave said, 'Look, you can see I'm busy. I have $1000 in my hand.'

But Jeff was adamant. 'Please, please, Dave, take a look at this.'

Dave looked up and saw that standing at the top of the ravine were 5000 red Indians in full battle gear, arrows arched.

Dave shook his head and said, 'Oh . . . my . . . God . . . we're going to be millionaires!'


'**D**o you believe in life after death?' the boss asked the blonde employee.

'Yes, sir,' the new recruit replied.

'Well, then, that makes everything just fine,' the boss went on, 'After you left early yesterday to go to your grandmother's funeral, she stopped in to see you . . .'


**A** blonde was staring really hard at a carton of orange juice. When I asked what she was she doing, she replied, 'Well, it says on the carton, "concentrate".'

There was a brunette jumping on the train tracks screaming, '21, 21, 21 . . .'

A blonde walked by and thought it looked fun so she jumped on the train tracks screaming, '21, 21, 21 . . .'

A train came.

The brunette jumped off the tracks.

The blond got hit.

The train passed.

The brunette jumped back onto the train tracks and started screaming, '22, 22, 22 . . .'

# BLONDE BLOKES

A woman and a man are involved in a bad car accident. Both cars are written off, but thankfully neither are hurt.

After they crawl out of their cars, the woman says, 'So you're a man; that's interesting. I'm a woman. Gee, just look at our cars! There's nothing left, but fortunately we are unhurt. This must be a sign from God that we should meet and be friends and live together for the rest of our days.'

Flattered, the blonde bloke replied, 'Oh yes, I agree with you completely! This must be a sign from God!'

The woman continued, 'And look at this, here's another miracle. My car is completely demolished but this bottle of wine didn't break. Surely God wants us to drink this wine and celebrate our good fortune.'

Then she hands the bottle to the man.

The man nods his head in agreement, opens it and drinks half the bottle and then hands it back to the woman.

The woman takes the bottle, immediately puts the cap back on and hands it back to the man.

The man asks, 'Aren't you having any?'

The woman replies, 'No. I think I'll just wait for the police.'

A blonde bloke is walking down the street with a pig under his arm.

He passes a person who asks, 'Where did you get that?'

The pig says, 'I won him in a raffle!'

## MEN LIKE BLONDES

Scientists for Health Canada suggest that drinking beer makes men act like blonde women.

To test the theory, 100 men were fed six pints of beer each, within a one hour period.

It was then observed that 100% of the men gained weight, talked excessively without making sense, became overly emotional, couldn't drive, failed to think rationally, argued over nothing and refused to apologise when they were wrong.

The blonde priest was having a heart-to-heart talk with a lapsed member of his flock, whose drinking of cheap cask wine invariably led to quarrelling with his neighbours and occasional shotgun blasts at some of them.

'Can't you see, Ben,' intoned the parson, 'That not one good thing comes out of this drinking?'

'Well, I sort of disagree there,' replied the drunk. 'It makes me miss the people I shoot at.'

## SEMINARS FOR BLONDE MEN

- You Can Do the Housework, Too.
- Understanding the Female Response to You Coming In Drunk at 4 am.
- Wonderful Laundry Techniques (formerly called Don't Wash My Silks).
- Parenting—Participation Doesn't End With Conception.
- Get A Life—Learn To Cook.

Bob, a travelling salesman, arrives at a small town late in the day, walks into the local bar, sits down and orders up a beer.

To his amazement, everyone in the bar is a blonde. They are having a wonderful time.

After a few moments, someone stands up and shouts, '28!' and the entire bar bursts into hysterical laughter.

Bob thinks this is strange, but goes back to his beer.

A few moments later someone else stands up and yells, '33!'

Once again, the bar bursts into fits of laughter. Some are rolling on the floor.

Bob shakes his head and goes back to his beer.

Soon, a third man stands up and shouts, 'Four!'

Again, everyone in the bar laughs, some uncontrollable in their mirth.

The completely confused Bob summons the bartender and asks what the hell all the laughing is about.

The bartender replies, 'See, pal, we're such a small town that everyone knows everyone and all of their jokes. So, to make life easier, we catalogued all of our gags. Instead of telling the whole joke, we just shout out its number and everyone knows what joke it is and we laugh.'

Bob listens carefully, nods and sits down.

More people stand up and shout numbers and eventually Bob cannot stand it any longer. Well-known as the life of the party back home, he has to join in.

Bob stands up and shouts, '41!'

Nobody laughs. There is stony silence. Bob sits down, shamefaced and embarrassed.

He summons up the bartender and says, 'What happened? No-one laughed.'

The bartender shakes his head and says, 'Buddy, it's not so much the joke, it's the way you tell it.'

'SHAAAYYYY, buddy, what's a 'Breathalyser?' asked a blonde drunk of his barman.

'That's a bag that tells you when you've drunk too much,' answered the barman.

'Ah hell, whaddya know? I've been married to one of those for years.'

Every night, Frank would go down to the liquor store, get a six-pack, bring it home and drink it while he watched TV.

One night, as he finished his last beer, the doorbell rang.

He stumbled to the door and found a six foot blonde cockroach standing there.

The bug grabbed him by the collar and threw him across the room, then left.

The next night, after he finished his fourth beer, the doorbell rang.

He walked slowly to the door and found the same huge blonde cockroach standing there.

The big bug punched him in the stomach, then left.

The next night, after Frank finished his first beer, the doorbell rang again.

The same six foot cockroach was standing there.

This time Frank was kneed in the groin and hit behind the ear as he doubled over in pain. Then the big bug left.

The fourth night Frank didn't drink at all.

The doorbell rang.

The cockroach was standing there.

The bug beat the snot out of Frank and left him in a heap on the living room floor.

The following day, Frank went to see his doctor.

He explained the events of the preceding four nights. 'I thought it might be the drink,' said Frank.

'But he belted me when I didn't have a beer.

'So, what can I do?' Frank pleaded.

'Not much,' the doctor replied. 'There's just a nasty bug going around.'

## SIGNS THAT YOU ARE TOO DRUNK OR TOO BLONDE WOULD BE . . .

- You lose arguments with inanimate objects.
- You have to hold onto the lawn to keep from falling off the earth.
- Your job is interfering with your drinking.
- Your doctor finds traces of blood in your alcohol stream.
- The back of your head keeps getting hit by the toilet seat.
- You sincerely believe alcohol to be the elusive fifth food group.
- Twenty-four hours in a day, 24 beers in a case— coincidence?—I think not!

- You can focus better with one eye closed.
- The parking lot seems to have moved while you were in the bar.
- Your twin sons are named Barley and Hops.
- Mosquitoes catch a buzz after attacking you.
- At AA meetings you begin, 'Hi, my name is . . . uh . . .'
- Your idea of cutting back is less salt.
- The whole bar says 'Hi' when you come in . . .

## ARE YOU A NEANDERTHAL BLONDE?

1. Do your beautiful blonde eyebrows meet in the middle?
2. Can you lock your knees in an upright position?
3. Got a chin?
4. How about a forehead?
5. Do you ever open beer bottles with your teeth?
6. Pigeon-toed?
7. Is your nickname 'Duke', 'Butch' or 'Animal'?

## TROUBLEMAKER GEORGE

**A** group of loud and rowdy blonde blokes was making a hell of a racket in the street after a big night on the booze.

It was in the wee small hours of the morning and the lady of the house flung open a window and shouted at them to keep quiet.

'Is this where George lives?' one of the drunks asked.

'Yes, it is,' the woman replied.

'Well then,' said the drunk, 'Could you come and pick him out so the rest of us can go home?'

## A BLONDE BLOKE'S OPINION OF HIS WIFE

**I** married Miss Right. I just didn't know her first name was Always.

**I** haven't spoken to my wife for 18 months—I don't like to interrupt her.

**A**ll wives are alike, but they have different faces so you can tell them apart.

**W**omen are like guns—keep one around long enough and you're going to want to shoot it.

**B**igamy is having one wife too many. Some say monogamy is the same.

**M**arriage is a three ring circus: engagement ring, wedding ring and suffering.

## HOW'S THAT?

A young man and his blonde manager go down to the red light district of town.

The manager is betting every person he meets that his young friend can screw and satisfy 100 women in a row, without pausing.

Bets are made and they agree that they'll meet the next day to complete the arrangement.

The next day, 100 women are lined up and the young Romeo drops his pants and begins the task at hand.

True to his word, he moves from one to the next, satisfying each one without pausing: 1 . . . 2 . . . 3 . . . on and on he goes . . . 49 . . . 50 . . . 51 . . .

He slows down somewhat, 83 . . . 84 . . . 85. But he is still moving from one to the next and the women are still satisfied: 97 . . . 98 . . . 99 . . .

But before he can get to the last woman he has a heart attack and dies.

The manager scratches his head and says, 'I don't understand it! It went perfectly at practice this morning!'

## IN A PICKLE

O ne day blonde Bill comes home absolutely ashen. His wife could see at once that something was seriously wrong. 'What's wrong, Bill?' she asked.

'Do you remember that I told you how I had this tremendous urge to put my penis in the pickle slicer?'

'Oh, Bill, you didn't.'

'Yes, I did.'

'My god, Bill, what happened?'

'I got fired.'

'No, Bill. I mean, what happened with the pickle-slicer?'

'Oh. She got fired too.'

A man walks up to a blonde woman in his office and tells her that her hair smells nice.

The blonde immediately goes into her supervisor's office and tells him that she wants to file a sexual harassment suit and explains why.

The supervisor is puzzled by this time and says, 'What's wrong with the co-worker telling you that your hair smells nice.'

The woman replies, 'He's a midget.'

## YOU KNOW THAT YOU HAVE MADE LOVE TO A BLONDE IF:

- Your mattress has turned into a giant sponge.
- It takes five minutes to un-knot your bodies.
- An earthquake of 7.4 on the Richter Scale is recorded in your area.
- The cat's exhausted from just watching you.
- A trampoline company has to come to adjust your bed springs.
- You've both gone down one clothing size.
- You cancel your chiropractic appointment. There's nothing left to adjust.
- You have to breathe into a brown paper bag.
- Boy, are you hungry!
- You're absolutely satisfied yet uncontrollably horny at the same time.

A man with his blonde hair and his face covered with a balaclava bursts into a sperm bank with a shotgun.

'Open the safe,' he yells at the girl behind the counter.

'But we're not a real bank,' she replies, 'We don't have any money, this is a sperm bank'.

'Don't argue, open the fucking safe or I'll blow your head off'

She obliges and once she's opened the safe door, the guy says, 'Take out one of the bottles and drink it'.

'But it's full of sperm!' she replies nervously.

'Don't argue, just drink it,' he says.

She prises the cap off and gulps it down.

'Take out another one and drink it too,' he demands.

She takes out another and drinks it as well.

Suddenly the guy pulls off the balaclava and to the girl's amazement it's her husband.

'There,' he says 'It's not that difficult is it!'

Joe sat as his dying wife's bedside. Her voice was little more than a whisper.

'Joe, darling,' she breathed, 'I've got a confession to make before I go. I . . . I'm the one who took the $10,000 from your safe. I spent it on a fling with your best friend, Charles. And it was I who forced your mistress to leave the city. And I am the one who reported your income-tax evasion to the tax office . . .'

'That's all right, dearest, don't give it a second thought,' whispered Joe. 'I'm the one who poisoned you.'

I was given the ultimatum three weeks ago. She said, 'It's me or your fishing.'

Gee I miss her.

A blonde bloke phones home from his office and tells his blonde wife: 'Something has just come up. I have a chance to go fishing for a week. It's the opportunity of a lifetime and we leave right away. So pack my clothes, my fishing equipment and especially my blue silk pyjamas. I'll be home in and hour to pick them up.'

He goes home in a hurry and grabs everything and rushes off.

A week later he returns.

His wife asks, 'Did you have a good trip, dear?'

He says, 'Oh yes it was great. But you forgot to pack my blue silk pyjamas.'

His wife smiles and says, 'Oh no, I didn't. I put them in your tackle box!'

A man met a beautiful blonde lady and he decided he wanted to marry her right away.

She said, 'But we don't know anything about each other.'

He said, 'That's all right, we'll learn about each other as we go along.'

So she consented. They were married and went on a honeymoon to a very nice resort. One morning they were lying by the pool, when he got up off of his towel, climbed up to the top of the 10 metre diving board and did a two and a half tuck, followed by three rotations in jack-knife position, where he straightened out and cut the water like a knife. After a few more demonstrations, he came back and lay down on the towel.

She said, 'That was incredible!'

He said, 'I used to be an Olympic diving champion. You see, I told you we'd learn more about ourselves as we went along.'

So she got up, jumped in the pool and started doing laps. After about thirty laps she climbed back out and lay down on her towel hardly out of breath.

He said, 'That was incredible! Were you an Olympic endurance swimmer?'

'No,' she said, 'I was a hooker in Venice and I worked both sides of the canal . . .'

## BLONDE DRIVER'S LAMENT

**D**riving to the office this morning on the motorway, I looked over to my right and there was a blonde in a brand new BMW doing 90 miles per hour, with her face up close to her rear view mirror, putting on her eyeliner!

I looked away for a couple of seconds and when I looked back she was halfway over in my lane still working on that makeup!

It scared me so much that I dropped my electric shaver, which knocked the bacon roll out of my other hand.

In all the confusion of trying to straighten out the car using my knees against the steering wheel, it knocked my mobile from my ear, which fell into the coffee between my legs, causing it to splash and burn so that I screamed, which made me drop the cigarette out of my mouth, ruined my shirt and disconnected an important call I was on at the time.

# BLONDES AND SEX . . .

A young blonde virgin decides she wants to learn a bit more about life so she packs her bags, bids farewell to her Aunty Maureen who has looked after her for years, and starts hitch-hiking to London.

Eventually, a large car pulls up, so in she gets.

Being a friendly sort, she starts chatting to the driver.

'And what do you do for a living?' she says.

'I'm a disc jockey,' he says, 'On the radio'.

'Oh my,' she says, 'Do you play requests because my Aunt Maureen will be ever so worried about me and if you could play a request and let her know that I'm all right, I will be most grateful.'

'Of course I will,' says the DJ, 'But you must do something for me first.'

'Okay,' she says.

So he pulls the car over and unzips his fly and pulls out his enormous erect penis.

'Put your lips down to that,' he says.

So she leans over, carefully grabs hold of his penis and shouts, 'HELLO, AUNTIE MAUREEN . . .'

Two blonde ladies of the night stroll into a department store.

They walk up to the perfume counter and pick up a sample bottle.

Sharon sprays it on her wrist and smells it, 'That's quite nice isn't it, don't you think Jacinta?'

'Yeah, what's it called?'

'Viens à moi.'

'VIENS A MOI, what the hell does that mean?'

At this stage the assistant offers some help. 'Viens à moi, ladies, is French for "come to me".'

Sharon, takes another sniff and offers her arm to Jacinta again saying, 'That doesn't smell like come to me, does that smell like come to you?'

A blonde goes into the drug store to buy some rubbers so that she can practice safe sex.

She walks up to the pharmacist and asks, 'How much for a box of rubbers?'

'They're $1 for a box of three,' he replies, 'Plus six cents for the tax.'

'Oh,' replies the blonde, 'I wondered how they kept them on!'

This blonde walks into a telephone office and tells the man behind the counter that there has been a family urgency and she has to immediately call her mother, who is holidaying in a remote part of Africa.

After looking up the charge list, the man says that such a call to such a remote place is not easy to set up and just three minutes on the phone would cost her $120.

The blonde is shocked, saying she just couldn't afford that much.

The man looks at her very kindly and says gently, 'Maybe we can work something out between us. Let's go to the back room.'

They go out the back, where the man tells her to get on her knees in front of him, which she does.

He says, 'Unzip my pants.'

She unzips his pants.

He says, 'Take it out.'

She takes it out.

He says, 'Put it to your lips.'

She puts it to her lips.

After waiting for a bit, with nothing happening, the man looks down and says 'Well, go ahead!'

The blonde looks up at him puzzled and then finally, slowly, holds it again to her mouth.

And says, 'Hello? Mum?'


Some blondes are gathered and the subject of conversation turns to sex and then birth control.

The first woman says, 'We're Catholic so we can't use birth control.'

The next woman says, 'I am too, but we use the rhythm method.'

The third woman says, 'We use the bucket and saucer method.'

'What the heck is the bucket and saucer method?' the others ask.

'Well, I'm five foot eleven . . . and my husband is five foot two.

'We make love standing up with him standing on a bucket. And when his eyes get big as saucers, I kick the bucket out from under him.'

A young fireman placed a ladder against the bedroom window of a burning house and rushed up.

Inside was a curvy blonde in a see-through nightie.

'Aha,' said he, 'You're the second pregnant girl I've rescued this year!'

'But I'm not pregnant,' the blonde indignantly exclaimed.

'You're not rescued yet either . . .'

A blonde takes a lover during the day, while her husband is out fishing. Her young son comes home early from school, so she puts him in the closet and shuts the door.

Her husband also comes home unexpectedly because it has started to get windy out on the bay, so she puts her lover in the closet, with the little boy.

The little boy says, 'Dark in here.'

The man says, 'Yes, it is.'

Boy, 'I have a baseball.'

Man, 'That's nice.'

Boy, 'Want to buy it?'

Man, 'No, thanks.'

Boy, 'My dad's outside.'

Man, 'Okay, how much?'

Boy, '$250.'

In the next few weeks, it happens again that the boy and the lover are in the closet together.

Boy, 'Dark in here.'

Man, 'Yes, it is.'

Boy, 'I have a baseball glove.'

The lover remembering the last time, asks the boy: 'How much?'

Boy, '$750.'

Man, 'Fine.'

A few days later, the father says to the boy.

'Grab your glove, let's go outside and have a catch.'

The boy says, 'I can't, I sold my baseball and my glove.'

The father asks, 'How much did you sell them for?'

Boy, '$1,000.'

The father says, 'That's terrible to overcharge your friends like that. That is way more than those two things cost. I'm going to take you to church and make you confess.'

They go to the church and the father makes the little boy sit in the confession booth and he closes the door.

The boy says, 'Dark in here.'

The priest says, 'Don't start that shit again . . .'

# BLONDES, BRUNETTES AND REDHEADS . . .

Three married couples—a blonde couple, a brunette couple and a redheaded couple—wanted to join the Orthodox Church of Sexual Repression.

Near the end of the interview, the priest informs them that before they can be accepted they will have to pass one small test.

They will have to abstain from all sex for a month. They all agree to try.

A month later they are having their final interview with the cleric.

He asks the redheaded old couple how they did. 'Well, it wasn't too hard. I spent a lot of time in the workshop and she has a garden so we had plenty of other things to do. We did okay,' the husband said.

'Very good, my children. You are welcome in the Church. And how well did you manage?' he asked the brunette couple.

'It was pretty difficult,' the husband answered. 'We thought about it all the time. We had to sleep in different beds and we prayed a lot. But we were celibate for the entire month.'

'Very good, my children. You are welcome in the Church. And how about you?' he asked the young blonde couple.

'Not too good, I'm afraid, Father. We did okay for the first week,' he said sheepishly. 'By the second week we were going crazy with lust. Then one day during the third week my wife dropped a head of lettuce and when she bent over to pick it up, I ... I weakened and took her right there.'

'I'm sorry my son, you are not welcome in the Church.'

'Yeah and we're not too welcome in the grocery department of Safeway anymore, either.'

Three women are about to be executed—a redhead, a brunette and a blonde.

The guard brings the redhead forward and the executioner asks if she has any last requests. She says no and the executioner shouts, 'Ready! Aim ...'

Suddenly the redhead yells, 'Earthquake!'

Everyone is startled and they all throw themselves on the ground for safety. When they look up the redhead has escaped.

The guard brings the brunette forward and the executioner asks if she has any last requests. She says no and the executioner shouts, 'Ready! Aim . . .'

Suddenly the brunette yells, 'Tornado!'

Again, everyone is startled and dives for cover. When they look up, the brunette has escaped.

By now the blonde has it all figured out.

The guard brings her forward and the executioner asks if she has any last requests. She says no and the executioner shouts, 'Ready! Aim . . .'

And the blonde yells, 'FIRE!'

E leven blondes and one brunette are hanging on a rope If one of them does not let go of the rope and sacrifice herself for the good of the others, it will break and they will all die.

The brunette says she will sacrifice herself and let go because the blondes are such good friends that they would all grieve too much if one of them was to die and wreck their lives.

She finishes her speech and the blondes are so touched by her generosity that all they begin to clap . . .

A blonde, a brunette and a redhead are running from a man and they run into a barn and they see three sacks in the corner.

They decide to hide in the three sacks.

The man comes in shortly after and seeing the sacks moving, he goes up to the first with the brunette in it and kicks it.

The brunette mimics a cat and says 'Meow,' and the man thinks there's a cat in there and leaves it alone.

He goes up to the second sack with the redhead in and kicks it.

The redhead mimics a dog and says 'Woof,' so the man thinks there's a dog in the sack and leaves it.

The man goes up to the final sack with the blonde in it and kicks it.

The blonde says, 'Potatoes!'

A brunette doing laundry asked her blonde friend to help her find a match for her sock.

The blonde replied, 'What for? Are you going to set it on fire!'

**Q.**　A blonde and a brunette both jump off a cliff at the same time. Which one will hit the bottom first?

**A.**　*The brunette, because the blonde has to ask for directions.*

One day three blonde sisters decided to jump in their car and drive over to Disneyland.

They lived a couple of hours drive away from Disneyland and they kept themselves entertained by telling each other jokes.

One of the sisters noticed a sign that read, 'Disneyland Park 3 Exits Ahead'.

They began to get excited.

They passed the first exit and they began to smile and laugh as they came closer to their destination.

They passed the second exit which read, 'Disneyland Up Ahead'.

They began to giggle and jump up and down like little girls.

Then they finally reached the third exit sign which read, 'Disneyland Left'.

Sadly, they said, 'Aw, shucks,' turned the car around and headed back home!

**A** redhead, a brunette and a blonde were at the fair and about to go on the helter-skelter when an old woman stepped in front of them.

'This is a magic ride,' she says. 'You will land in whatever you shout out on the way down.'

'I'm game for this,' says the redhead and slides down the helter-skelter shouting 'Gold!' at the top of her voice.

Sure enough, when she hit the bottom she found herself surrounded by thousands of dollars worth of gold coins.

The brunette went next and shouted 'Silver!' at the top of her voice.

At the bottom she landed in more silver coinage than she could carry.

The blonde went off and, launching herself from the top of the slide shouted 'Weeeeeee!'

# BLONDE WORKMEN AND WOMEN

The blonde bricklayer was doing some work on the fireplace in Mr Cabot's expensive home.

He was much impressed by the moose-head over the fireplace.

'It's a beautiful animal, Mr Cabot,' he said, 'The biggest I've ever seen.'

'Yes,' said Mr Cabot, 'That moose was a fighter among all moose. I tracked him for over two days and it took six men nearly 30 hours to get him back to our jeep.'

Shaking his blonde curls in admiration, the bricklayer said, 'Wow, what a great hunter and what a huge catch. Do you mind if I go into the next room and see the rest of him?'

A blonde workman on a building site was going up and down the ladder, with the same hod of bricks each time.

One of his friends said, 'What's the idea, Tom?'

Blonde Tom replied, 'I've had an argument with the foreman and I'm fooling him. He thinks I'm working!'

Judi, the blonde, runs crying into the office.

'What's wrong?' gasps her best friend Carol.

'It's my boyfriend,' gushes Judi. 'He was working on the engine under the hood of his car when the lid came down and cut off a finger!'

'My god,' shrieks Carol. 'Did it amputate his WHOLE finger!?'

'No thank goodness,' sniffs Judi. 'But it was the one just next to it!'


'**W**ell, Mrs. Smith, so you really want a divorce?' the solicitor questioned his blonde client. 'Tell me about it. Do you have a grudge?'

'Oh, no,' replied Mrs. Smith. 'We have a carport.'

The solicitor tried again. 'Well, does the man beat you up?'

'No, no,' said Mrs. Smith, looking puzzled. 'I'm always first out of bed.'

Still hopeful, the solicitor tried once again.

'What I'm trying to find out are what grounds you have.'

'We live in a flat—don't even have a window box, let alone grounds.'

'Mrs. Smith,' the solicitor said in considerable exasperation, 'You need a reason that the court can consider. What is the reason for you seeking this divorce?'

'Well,' said the blonde lady, 'It's because the man can't hold an intelligent conversation.'


**A** big muscle-bound brickie sauntered into a bar and shouted, 'Which one of you is Martin McGirk?'

A little blonde bloke standing by the bar said, 'That's me.'

The big guy walked over to him and punched him in the mouth.

The little feller started laughing, so the big guy hit him again and he fell down, still laughing.

The hulk could not bear it. 'Why are you still laughing?' he roared.

'The joke is on you!' said the little man. 'I'm not Martin McGirk at all!'

**A** blonde bloke was trapped in a bog and seemed a goner when a big man wandered by.

'Help!' the blonde bloke shouted, 'I'm sinking!'

'Don't worry,' assured the big man. 'I'm the strongest man around and I'll pull you right out of there.'

He leaned out and grabbed the blonde bloke's hand and pulled and pulled, to no avail.

After two more unsuccessful attempts, the big man said to the blonde bloke, 'I can't do it. I'll have to get some help.'

As he was leaving, the blonde bloke called, 'Do you think it will help if I pull me feet out of the stirrups . . .?

**A** blonde walks into a pharmacy and asks the pharmacist for a bottom deodorant.

'Sorry, we don't sell bottom deodorant,' the pharmacist replies, struggling to keep from laughing.

'But I always buy it here,' the blonde says. 'I bought one last month'.

Thinking quickly, the pharmacist suggests, 'I don't know what you bought before, may be you can bring in the empty container next time.'

'Sure,' the blonde replies. 'I'll bring it with me tomorrow.'

The next day, the blonde walks into the shop again and hands the pharmacist an almost-empty deodorant stick.

'This is just a normal deodorant,' the pharmacist tells the blonde, 'You use it under your arms'.

'No, it is not,' the blonde answers, 'It says so here, "To apply, push up bottom".'

**A** blonde received a certificate for helicopter flying lessons for his birthday.

One day he was bored and decided to take advantage of the opportunity.

When he arrived at the place, the man said, 'Well, there's only one helicopter here and it only has one seat, if I show you how to do it, do you mind going up solo?'

'Oh of course! I can handle it,' the blonde replied.

Well, he showed him the inner-workings of the helicopter and sent him on his way, only asking that he radio in every 400 ft just to make sure everything was going smoothly.

At 400 ft he radioed in saying, 'Wow! This is so much fun!'

At 800 ft he radioed in again saying, 'This is pretty easy, I can do this all day!'

At 1200 ft he didn't radio at all.

The instructor waited and waited and didn't hear from the blonde!

Seconds later he heard a crash in the field next to the station.

He ran out to see what happened—the blonde had crashed!

But luckily he had survived.

The instructor pulled him out of the wreckage. 'What happened?' he exclaimed.

'Well, I was doing fine,' said the blonde.

'But I started to get cold, so I just turned off the big fan!'


A blonde bloke was selling his house and put the matter in an agent's hands.

The agent wrote up a sales blurb for the house that made wonderful reading.

After the blonde bloke read it, he turned to the agent and asked, 'Have I got all you say there?'

The agent said, 'Certainly you have. Why do you ask?'

Replied the blonde, 'Cancel the sale. It's too good to part with.'

A ventriloquist is half way through his stand-up routine, the patter between himself and his little doll.

He's going through his usual run of silly blonde jokes when a big blonde woman in the fourth row stands on her chair and says,

'Okay jerk, I've heard just about enough of your denigrating blonde jokes. What makes you think you can stereotype women that way? What do a person's physical attributes have to do with their worth as a human being? It's guys like you who keep women like me from being respected at work and in my community, of reaching my full potential as a person, because you and your kind continue to perpetuate discrimination against not only blondes but women at large— all in the name of humour.'

Flustered, the ventriloquist begins to apologise, when the blonde cuts him off, 'You stay out of this, mister, I'm talking to that little bastard on your knee!'

The blonde's attempt on Mount Everest was a valiant effort, but it failed.

He ran out of scaffolding.

It is the first time a blonde has been on an aeroplane and she is understandably very excited and tense.

As soon as she boards the plane, a Boeing 747, she started jumping from seat to seat with excitement shouting, 'BOEING! BOEING!! BOEING! BO . . .'

The pilot hears the disturbance and emerges from the cockpit.

He sees the blonde trampling the other travellers and shouts 'BE SILENT!'

There is suddenly pin-drop silence.

Everyone on the flight is looking at the blonde and the angry pilot.

She stares at the pilot in silence for a moment, then concentrating really hard, she begins shouting, 'OEING! OEING! OEING! OE . . .'

Two blondes were out fishing and the boat's motor quit.

One blonde says to the other, 'What are we going to do now?'

The first says, 'We'll just have to wait for help.'

They wait.

After two days they are 40 kilometres from the coast and come across a bottle.

They open the bottle and out pops a genie who offers to grant them one wish.

Quick as a flash the first blonde says, 'Turn the sea into champagne!'

Immediately the sea is bubbling with champagne.

The second says, 'You stupid fool! Now we'll have to pee in the boat!'

While holidaying in Ireland, a tourist went into a small town in County Tipperary and was surprised at the apparent disregard for parking restrictions.

Double yellow lines were treated simply as decorative edges to the footpath.

He mentioned this to a blonde shopkeeper.

'You should be here on a Thursday,' he said. 'That's the parking officer's day off.'

Two blond blokes agreed to settle their dispute by a fight and it was understood that whoever wanted to quit should say 'Enough'.

One got the other down and was hammering him unmercifully when the first blond called out several times, 'Enough!'

As the first paid no attention, but kept on administering punishment, a bystander said, 'Why don't you let him up? Don't you hear him say that he's had enough?'

'I do,' says the first, 'But he's such a liar, you can't believe him.'

A blonde walks into an electronics store and says, 'I'd like to buy that television please.' The salesperson replies, 'I'm sorry. We don't sell to blondes here.'

The blonde goes home and dyes her hair brown.

A few days later she returns to the store, again asking to buy the TV.

'I told you, we don't sell to blondes. Please go home!' the salesperson tells her.

The blonde goes home, shaves her head and puts on a baseball cap.

She waits a few days once again goes to the shop to buy the television.

'We just don't sell to blondes here! It's store policy. Please, give up! Go home!' the salesperson exclaims.

'Look I dyed my hair and you still knew I was blonde. I shaved my head and wore a hat, but you still knew I was blonde! How do you know?' she asks exasperated.

The salesperson points to the item she wants. 'Well, first of all, that's a microwave . . .'

A blonde was trying to sell her car, but she was having a lot of problems selling it as it had 300,000 kilometres on the clock.

She was lamenting her problem one day when a brunette workmate pulled her aside.

'There is a possibility to make the car easier to sell, but it's not legal,' the brunette said.

'That doesn't matter,' replied the blonde, 'If I only can sell the car.'

'Okay,' said the brunette. 'Here is the address of a friend of mine. He owns a car repair shop. Tell him I sent you and he will turn the counter in your car back to 50,000 kilometres. That will make your car easier to sell.'

The following weekend, the blonde made the trip to the mechanic.

A few weeks later the brunette asked the blonde, 'Did you sell your car?'

'No,' replied the blonde, 'Why should I? It only has 50,000 kilometres on it.'

A blonde was driving down the highway when she saw another blonde sitting in the middle of a field trying to row a boat.

'It's blondes like her that give blondes like me a bad name,' she thought.

Exasperated, she stopped her car got out and yelled, 'Look at you. You're trying to row a boat in the middle of a field! If I could swim, I'd come over and kick your butt!'

Two blonde blokes landed themselves a job at a sawmill. Just before morning tea one yelled, 'Help! I lost me finger!'

'Have you now?' says the first blonde. 'And how did you do it?'

'I just touched this big spinning thing here like this . . . Darn! There goes another one!'

Three blondes are attempting to change a light bulb. Finally, one of them decides to call 000.

Blonde: Help! We need help. We are three blondes changing a light bulb.

Operator: Hmm! You put in a fresh bulb?

Blonde: Yes.

Operator: The power in the house is on?

Blonde: Of course.

Operator: And the switch is on?

Blonde: Yes, yes.

Operator: And the bulb still won't light up?

Blonde: No, it's working fine.

Operator: Then what's the problem?

Blonde: We got dizzy spinning the ladder around and we all fell and hurt ourselves.

Tired of the blonde-bashing, it all becomes too much for one blonde who decides to commit suicide by hanging herself from a tree in the park.

A few days later a man walks past the tree with his dog and spots her hanging from the tree.

He asks the blonde what she is doing and she replies, 'I'm hanging myself.'

'You're supposed to put the noose around your neck, not your waist,' said the onlooker.

'I tried that,' replied the blonde, 'But I couldn't breathe.'

**D**own on her luck, a blonde decides to go to the swish part of town and earn some extra money doing some handyman jobs.

At the first house she comes to, she rings the doorbell and asks if there are any odd jobs she could do.

'Well, actually,' the man replied, 'We need the porch painted. How much would you charge?'

The blonde said she felt $50 was fair.

'Okay. The ladders, paint and other tools you need are in the garage,' he replied.

When the man closed the door, his wife who had overheard the conversation, asked him, 'Only $50? Does she realise that the porch goes all the way around the house?'

The man replied, 'She must have, she was standing right on it.'

About 45 minutes later the doorbell rings again and the man is surprised to find his painter standing there.

She tells him that she's done and says that she even had enough paint to do two coats. As the man is reaching into his wallet to pay her, the blonde says, 'Oh and by the way, that isn't a Porsche—it's a Ferrari.'

**L**ady Crofton-Smythe was giving an upper-crust party and had hired Lena, a blonde girl who had recently come to London and was working as a maid.

As Lena was setting up the tea service, Lady Crofton-Smythe told her to be certain that there were sugar tongs available.

Lena had never heard of sugar tongs and asked the Lady what they were and why they were used.

Lady Crofton-Smythe, always happy to enlighten the unenlightened, told Lena that the problem lay with the gentlemen, who would go to the loo and to do what they needed to do, had to touch things which were less than acceptably sanitary. Yes, even the nobility was subject to this masculine frailty.

'Well, Ma'am, I have never seen anything like this,' blonde Lena said, impressed.

After the guests had begun arriving that evening, Lady Crofton-Smythe was dismayed and infuriated not to see any sugar tongs on the tea service.

Lena, trembling, came quickly in answer to the Lady's angry shout.

'But . . . but, m'Lady, I put the tongs out just as you told me to.'

Her furious employer pointed to the tea table, devoid of tongs. 'Then where are they, young woman?'

'Why, they're in the loo, of course!'


**A** blonde was walking along, when she looked up to see a bird flying overhead. Suddenly, the bird drops a load when it is directly over her.

The blonde says, 'Good thing I had my mouth open or that would've hit me right in the face!'


**A** blonde and a brunette were watching the news when they saw a man at the top of a building threatening to jump off.

The brunette said, 'I bet you $50 he's going to jump off, what do you say?'

The blonde agreed.

They continued watching until the man jumped off the building.

The blonde hands over the $50 and says, 'Good work.'

The brunette takes the money but in a few minutes guiltily admits, 'I'm sorry, here's your $50 back, I saw the earlier showing of the news and I knew the man was going to jump off.'

'Don't worry,' said the blonde 'I saw it too. I just didn't think he'd do it again.'

A blonde was down on her luck.
In order to raise some money, she decided to kidnap a kid and hold him for ransom.

She went to the playground, grabbed a kid, took him behind a tree.

She wrote a note saying, 'I have kidnapped your kid. Tomorrow morning, put $10,000 in a paper bag and put it under the gum tree next to the slide on the north side of the playground. Signed, Blonde.'

The blonde then taped the note to the kid's shirt and sent him home to show to his parents.

The next morning the blonde checked and sure enough, a paper bag was sitting beneath the gum tree.

The blonde opened the bag and found the $10,000 with a note that said, 'How could you do this to a fellow blonde?'

Newly arrived in Boston, the blonde immigrant called his brother back home.

'It's amazing in these American cities. They're so rich! On most every street, they've got glass outhouses, with telephones in them!'

Two telephone company crews were putting up telephone poles.

At the end of the day, the company foreman asked the first crew how many poles they had put in the ground. 'Fifteen,' was the answer.

'Not bad, not bad at all,' the foreman said.

Turning to the blonde crew he asked how many they had put in.

'Four,' was the reply.

'Four?' the foreman yelled. 'The others did fifteen and you only did four?'

'Yes,' replied the leader of the blonde group, 'But look at how much of each one they left sticking out of the ground . . .'

**I** once met a girl who was so blonde that for our first date she told me to meet her at the corner of 'WALK' and 'DON'T WALK.'

**A** blonde bloke finds a Genie lamp and rubs it.
Out comes the Genie and asks, 'Master, you have released me from the lamp and I grant you three wishes, what would you like?'

The blonde bloke scratches his head, then answers, 'A bottle of Guinness that never gets empty.'

'Granted master,' retorts the Genie and produces the bottle. The blonde bloke is delighted and gets drunk on this one magic Guinness bottle for weeks. Then he remembers that he has two other wishes.

He rubs the lamp again and the Genie appears. 'Yes master, you have two more wishes, what would you like?'

'You know that magic, never-ending Guinness bottle,' he asks the Genie. 'Well, for my final two wishes, I'd like another two of them . . .'

**T** wo blondes opened a swimming pool.
Soon after they put up a sign at the gate:
'Due to a water shortage, only Lane One and Lane Four will be open. Thank you.'

**A** secret agent was sent to Ireland to pick up some very sensitive information from a blonde agent called Murphy.

His instructions were to walk around town using a code phrase until he met his fellow agent.

He found himself on a desolate country road and finally ran into a farmer.

'Hello,' said the agent, 'I'm looking for a man called Murphy.'

'Well you're in luck,' said the farmer, 'As it happens, there's a village right over the hill, where there's a butcher called Murphy, the baker is named Murphy and three widows are called Murphy. In fact my name is Murphy.'

'Aha,' thought the agent, 'Here's my man.'

So he whispered the secret code. 'The sun is shining . . . the grass is growing . . . the cows are ready for milking.'

'Oh,' said the farmer, 'You'll be looking for Murphy the spy—he's in the village over that other hill.'

Three girls are walking in a magical forest. Suddenly, a witch comes out of the woods and tells them, 'Each of you has to say one good thing about herself. If you lie, I will make you disappear!'

The first girl, a brunette, says, 'I think I am a very kind and thoughtful person'.

'Poof!' and she disappears.

The second girl, a redhead, says, 'I think I am very sexy'.

'Poof!' and she also disappears.

The third girl, a blonde, says, 'Well, I think . . .'

'Poof!' and she is gone . . .

Three blondes walk into a forest and soon find a pair of tracks.

The first blonde says, 'I think they're deer tracks.'

The second blonde says, 'No, I think they're bear tracks.'

The third blonde says, 'You're both wrong! They're bird tracks!'

Then they got hit by a train.

Two blondes are walking down a road. One has a large sports bag.

First blonde, 'What have you got in that bag?'

Second blonde, 'Chickens.'

First blonde, 'If I can guess how many chickens you've got in that bag, can I have one of them?'

Second blonde, 'If you can guess how many chickens I've got in this bag, you can have BOTH of them!'

First blonde, 'Well, I think you've got three . . .'


A girl came skipping home from school one day.

'Mummy, Mummy,' she yelled, 'We were counting today and all the other kids could only count to four, but I counted to 10. See? One, two, three, four, five, six, seven, eight, nine, ten!'

'Very good,' said her mother.

'Is it because I'm blonde?' the girl said.

'Yes, it's because you're blonde,' said the mum.

The next day the girl came skipping home from school.

'Mummy, Mummy,' she yelled, 'we were saying the alphabet today and all the other kids could only say it to D, but I said it to G. See? A, B, C, D, E, F, G!'

'Very good,' said her mother.

'Is it because I'm blonde, Mummy?'

'Yes, it's because you're blonde.'

The next day the girl came skipping home from school.

'Mummy, Mummy,' she yelled, 'We were in gym class today and when we showered, all the other girls had flat chests, but I have these!'

And she lifted her tank top to reveal a pair of 36Cs.

'Very good,' said her embarrassed mother.

'Is it because I'm blonde, Mummy?'

'No, honey, it's because you're 24.'

**A** blonde is walking down the street with her shirt open, exposing one of her breasts.

A policeman approaches her and says, 'Excuse me, are you aware that I could arrest you for indecent exposure?'

'Why, officer?' asks the blonde.

'Because your shirt is open and your breast is exposed.'

'Oh my goodness,' exclaims the blonde, 'I left my baby on the tram!'

**O** ne cold winter day, a blonde decides she wants to take up ice fishing.

When she gets to the pond, she begins to cut a hole in the ice.

As she does, she hears a voice. 'There's no fish there.'

Puzzled, the blonde picks up her stuff and cuts another hole a few feet away.

Again, she hears the voice. 'There's no fish there . . .'

The blonde is confused, but still determined.

About 10 feet away, she begins to cut another ice hole. 'There's no fish there,' she hears.

She immediately turns her head to the sky and says, 'Is that you, God?'

'No! I'm the manager of this ice skating rink . . .'

**O** ne day, two blonde fellows, Jamie and Alan, were out fishing.

A funeral service passes over the bridge they're fishing by and Alan takes off his hat and puts it over his heart.

He does this until the funeral service passes by.

Jamie then said, 'Gee Alan, I didn't know you had it in you!'

Alan replied, 'It's the least I could do. After all, I was married to her for 30 years.'

**A** man was surf fishing along the beach when he found a
bottle.

He looked around but didn't see anyone so he opened it

A genie appeared and thanked the man for letting him out.

The genie said, 'I am so grateful to get out of that bottle that
I will grant you any wish, but I can only grant one.'

The man thought for a while and finally said, 'I have always
wanted to go to Hawaii and fish along the beautiful beaches of
Hawaii. I've never been able to go because I cannot fly.
Airplanes are much too frightening for me. On a boat, I see all
that water and I become very claustrophobic. So I wish for a
road to be built from here to Hawaii.'

The genie thought for a few minutes and finally said, 'No, I
don't think I can do that. Just think of all the work involved.
Consider all the pylons needed to hold up a highway and how
deep they would have to go to reach the bottom of the ocean.
Imagine the amount of pavement needed. No, that really is just
too much to ask.'

The man thought for a few minutes and then told the
genie, 'There is one other thing I have always wanted. I would
like to be able to understand my beautiful blonde wife. What
makes her laugh and cry, why is she temperamental, why is
she so difficult to get along with, when does she want
attention and when doesn't she. Basically, what makes my
beautiful blonde wife tick.'

The genie thought for a while and said, 'So, do you want
two lanes or four . . . ?'


**A** man was downing his drinks faster than usual when the
man on the barstool next to him said, 'What's wrong?'

The first man said, 'I'm drinking to the memory of my
beautiful blonde wife. She was a saint on earth. She went to
church every single morning, spent her days reading and

quoting the Scriptures, sang hymns and psalms all evening, filled our house with religious statues and paintings and invited priests and nuns to dinner three times a week.'

'She sounds like an angel,' the second man commented. 'I suppose the good Lord took her early to Himself.'

'No,' the first man replied, 'I strangled her.'

Two blondes rented a fishing boat and were having a great day catching fish.

The first blonde said, 'This is such a great spot, we need to mark it so we can come back.'

The second blonde proceeded to put a mark on the side of the boat.

The first blonde asked, 'What are you doing?'

The second blonde replied, 'Marking the spot.'

'Don't be stupid,' the first blonde said. 'What if we don't get the same boat next time?'

The local District Judge who was a blonde had given the defendant a lecture on the evils of drink.

But in view of the fact that this was the first time the man had been drunk and incapable, the case was dismissed on payment of $20 costs.

'Now don't let me ever see your face again,' said the Justice sternly as the defendant turned to go.

'I'm afraid I can't promise that, sir,' said the released man.

'And why not?'

'Because I'm the barman at your regular pub!'

Once upon a time in the kingdom of Heaven, God went missing for seven days.

Eventually, Michael the Archangel found him.

He inquired of God, 'Where were you?'

God sighed a deep sigh of satisfaction and proudly pointed downwards through the clouds. 'Look son, look what I'm making.'

Archangel Michael looked puzzled and said, 'What is it?'

God replied, 'It's another planet, but I'm putting Life on it. I've named it Earth and there's going to be a balance between everything on it. For example, there's North America and South America. North America is going to be rich and blonde and South America is going to be poor and dark haired and the narrow bit joining them—that's going to be a hot spot. Now look over here. I've put a continent of blondes in the north and another one of blacks in the south.'

And then the archangel said, 'And what's that green dot there?'

And God said, 'Ah that's the Emerald Isle—that's a very special place. That's going to be the most glorious spot on earth; beautiful mountains, lakes, rivers, streams and an exquisite coastline. These people here are going to be great adventurers and they're going to be found travelling the world. They'll be playwrights and poets and singers and songwriters. And I'm going to give them this black liquid which they're going to go mad on and for which people will come from the far corners of the earth to imbibe.'

Michael the Archangel gasped in wonder and admiration but then seeming startled, proclaimed, 'Hold on a second, what about the *balance*? You said there was going to be a balance!'

God winked and replied wisely. 'Wait until you see the neighbours I'm going to give them . . .'

**B**ack in the Wild West, there are two blonde cowboys, Frank and Jim.

One day, the two are enjoying a drink in the local saloon, when a man walks into the bar with an Indian's head under his arm.

The barman shakes his hand and says, 'I hate Indians; last week the bastards burnt my barn to the ground, assaulted my wife and killed my children.'

He then adds, 'If any man brings me the head of an Indian, I'll give him one thousand dollars.'

The two blondes looked at each other and walk out of the bar and go hunting for an Indian.

They find one and Frank throws a rock which hits the Indian right on the head.

The Indian falls off his horse, but lands way down a ravine. The two blondes make their way down the ravine where Frank pulls out a knife ready to claim their trophy.

Jim calls urgently, 'Frank, take a look at this.'

Frank replies, 'Not now, I'm busy.'

Jim tries again with more panic in his voice and says, 'I really think you should look at this.'

Frank says, 'Look, you can see I'm busy? I have a thousand dollars in my hand!'

But Jim is adamant. 'Please, please, Frank, take a look at this.'

Frank looks up and sees that standing at the top of the ravine are ten thousand red Indians in full battle gear, their bows and arrows aimed at them.

Frank just shakes his head and says, 'Oh . . . my . . . God . . . we're going to be millionaires!'

A woman hired a contractor to repaint the interior of her house. The woman walked the man through the second floor of her home and told him what colours she wanted for each room.

As they walked through the first room, the woman said, 'I think I would like this room in a cream colour.'

The contractor wrote on his clipboard, walked to the window, opened it and yelled out, 'Green side up!' He then closed the window and continued following the woman to the next room.

The woman looked confused, but proceeded with her tour. 'In this room, I was thinking of an off blue.'

Again, the contractor wrote this down, went to the window, opened it and yelled out, 'Green side up!'

This baffled the woman, but she was hesitant to say anything.

In the next room, the woman said she would like it painted in a light rose colour.

And once more, the contractor walked over, opened the window and yelled, 'Green side up!'

Struck with curiosity, the woman mustered up the nerve to ask, 'Why do you keep yelling "Green side up" out my window every time I tell you the colour I would like the room?'

The contractor replied, 'Because, across the street, I have a crew of blondes laying instant lawn . . .'

**B**oyfriend: 'Why do you never scream my name when you have an orgasm?'

**Blonde:** 'Because you are never there.'

**T**wo blonde carpenters were working on a house. The one who was nailing down siding would reach into his nail pouch, pull out a perfectly good nail and either toss it over his shoulder or nail it in.

The other, figuring this was worth looking into, asked, 'Why are you throwing those nails away?'

The first explained, 'If I pull a nail out of my pouch and it's pointed toward me, I throw it away 'cause it's defective. If it's pointed toward the house, then I nail it in!'

The second blonde got completely upset and yelled, 'You moron! The nails pointed toward you aren't defective! They're for the other side of the house!'

On a plane bound for New York, the flight attendant approached a blonde sitting in the first class section and requested that she move to economy since she did not have a first class ticket.

The blonde replied, 'I'm blonde, I'm beautiful, I'm going to New York and I'm not moving.'

Not wanting to argue with a customer, the flight attendant asked the co-pilot to speak with her.

He went to talk with the woman asking her to please move out of the first class section.

Again, the blonde replied, 'I'm blonde, I'm beautiful, I'm going to New York and I'm not moving.'

The co-pilot returned to the cockpit and asked the captain what should he do. The captain said, 'I'm married to a blonde. I know how to handle this.'

He went to the first class section and whispered in the blonde's ear. She immediately jumped up and ran to the economy section mumbling to herself, 'Why didn't anyone just say so?'

Surprised, the flight attendant and the co-pilot asked what he said to her that finally convinced her to move from her seat.

He said, 'I told her the first class section wasn't going to New York . . .'

## SHE WAS SO BLONDE THAT:

- She sent me a fax with a stamp on it.
- She tried to put M&Ms in alphabetical order.
- She thought a quarterback was a refund.
- If you gave her a penny for intelligence, you'd get change back.
- She tripped over a cordless phone.
- She took a ruler to bed to see how long she slept.

- At the bottom of the application where it says 'Sign here', she put 'Sagittarius'.
- If she spoke her mind, she'd probably be speechless.
- She studied for a blood test—and failed.
- It takes her two hours to watch 60 Minutes.
- She sold the car for petrol money.
- When she took you to the airport and saw the sign that said 'Airport Left', she turned around and went home.
- In the space on the form that said 'Do not write here', she put 'Okay'.

**D**id you hear about the figure-conscious blonde who had square boobs?

She forgot to take the tissues out of the box.

# IN THE WORKPLACE

**T**hen there was the blonde working at Reception.

A fellow worker came up and said, 'Would you like to buy a raffle ticket? Janice in Production died suddenly last week. It's for her husband and four children.'

'No thanks,' the blonde says. 'I've already got a husband and two kids of my own.'

## DEFINITIONS FOR A BLONDE

**A**utomobile    A mechanical device that runs up hills and runs people down.

**B**rain    The apparatus with which we think that we think.

**F**airy Tales    Horror stories for children.

**J**ury    Twelve people who determine which client has the better lawyer.

## NOTICE TO ALL EMPLOYEES

This is a great trick to play on all the blondes at the office. You may also catch the feeble minded out as a bonus.

A Restroom Trip Policy will be established to provide a more consistent method of accounting for each employee's restroom time and ensuring equal opportunity for all employees.

Under this policy a 'Restroom Trip Bank' (RTB) will be established for each employee. The first day of each month, employees will be given twenty (20) RTB credits.

These credits may be accumulated indefinitely.

Within two weeks, the entrance doors to all restrooms will be equipped with personnel identification stations and computer-linked voice print recognition devices.

Each employee must provide two copies of voice prints— one normal and one under stress.

Employees should acquaint themselves with the stations during the initial introduction period.

If an employee's RTB balance reaches zero, the doors to the restroom will not unlock for that employee's voice until the first of the next month.

In addition, all restroom stalls are being equipped with timed paper roll retractors and pressure sensitive seats. If the stall is occupied for more than three minutes, an alarm will sound. Thirty seconds after the sounding of the alarm, the roll of paper will retract into the wall, the toilet will automatically flush and the stall door will open. If the stall remains occupied, your picture will be taken.

The picture will then be posted on the bulletin board and the first of no more than two official warnings will be issued. If a person's picture appears for a third time, it will be grounds for immediate termination.

All supervisors have received advanced training on this policy. If you have any questions, please ask your supervisor.

**A** blonde, a brunette and a redhead all work at the same office for a female boss who always goes home early.

'Hey, girls,' says the brunette, 'Let's go home early tomorrow. She'll never know.'

So the next day, they all leave right after the boss does.

The brunette gets some extra gardening done, the redhead goes to a bar and the blonde goes home to find her husband having sex with the female boss!

She quietly sneaks out of the house and returns at her normal time.

'That was fun,' says the brunette next day. 'We should do it again sometime.'

'No way,' says the blonde. 'I almost got caught.'

**O** ne day an out of work blonde mime is visiting the zoo and attempts to earn some money as a street performer.

As soon as he starts to draw a crowd, a zoo keeper grabs him and drags him into his office.

The zoo keeper explains to the mime that the zoo's most popular attraction, a gorilla, has died suddenly and the keeper fears that attendance at the zoo will fall off.

He offers the mime a job to dress up as the gorilla until they can get another one.

The mime accepts.

So the next morning the mime puts on the gorilla suit and enters the cage before the crowd comes.

He discovers that it's a great job.

He can sleep all he wants, play and make fun of people and he draws bigger crowds than he ever did as a mime.

However, eventually the crowds tire of him and he tires of just swinging on tyres.

He begins to notice that the people are paying more attention to the lion in the cage next to his.

Not wanting to lose the attention of his audience, he climbs to the top of his cage, crawls across a partition and dangles from the top to the lion's cage.

Of course, this makes the lion furious, but the crowd loves it.

At the end of the day the zoo keeper comes and gives the mime a raise for being such a good attraction.

This goes on for some time. The mime keeps taunting the lion, the crowds grow larger and his salary keeps going up.

Then one terrible day when he is dangling over the furious lion, he slips and falls into the lion enclosure.

The mime is terrified.

The lion gathers itself and prepares to pounce.

The mime is so scared that he begins to run round and round the cage with the lion close behind.

Finally, the mime starts screaming and yelling, 'Help, Help me!' but the lion is quick and pounces.

The blonde mime soon finds himself flat on his back looking up at the angry lion,

'Shut up you idiot!' hisses the lion, 'Do you want to get us both fired?'

The little sexy blonde housewife was built so well the TV repairman couldn't keep his eyes off of her.

Every time she came in the room, he'd nearly jerk his neck right out of joint looking at her.

When he'd finished, she paid him and said, 'I'm going to make an unusual request. But you have to first promise me you'll keep it a secret.'

The repairman quickly agreed and she went on.

'Well, it's kind of embarrassing to talk about, but while my husband is a kind, decent man, he has a certain physical weakness. A certain disability. Now, I'm a woman and you're a man . . .'

The repairman salivated in anticipation, 'Yes, yes!'

'And since I've been wanting to ever since you came in the door . . .'

'Yes, yes!'

'Would you please help me move the refrigerator?'

**A** man was eating in a restaurant and he dropped his spoon. The blonde waiter was immediately at his table and took another spoon out of his pocket and gave it to the man.

The man thanked him and took a sip of his soup and then asked, 'Excuse me, but why do all the waiters have spoons in their pockets?'

The waiter said, 'Well sir, a time and motion survey in our restaurant showed that 1 in 4 customers drop their spoon just like you, so we always have a spare spoon on hand so we can give it to the customer so that he is not eating with the dirty one. It saves time as the waiter does not have to go back to the kitchen to retrieve a clean spoon. The management prides itself in the efficiency of the staff.'

As the waiter walks back to the kitchen, the man noticed that there was a string hanging from his fly and the man said, 'Excuse me but why do you and all the other waiters, have a string hanging out of your flies?'

The blonde waiter said, 'Well sir, a survey in our restaurant showed that the waiters can save time and serve more customers, if we do not wash our hands after using the toilet. So we use the string tied to our penises to pull it out of our trousers so we don't get our hands dirty.'

Then the man took another sip of his soup and replied,

'That's all very well, but how do you get it back in again?'

'Well I don't know about the others,' replied the waiter, 'But, personally speaking, I use the spoon . . .'


**A** site foreman had ten very lazy men working for him, so one day he decided to trick them into doing some work for a change.

'I've got a really easy job today for the laziest one among you,' he announced. 'Will the laziest man please put his hand up.'

Nine hands went up.

'Why didn't you put your hand up?' he asked the tenth man who was a blonde.

'Too much trouble,' came the reply.

Two car salesmen were sitting at the bar.

One complained to the other, 'Boy, business sucks. If I don't sell more cars this month, I'm going to lose my damn ass.'

Then he noticed a beautiful blonde sitting two stools away.

Immediately, he apologised for his bad language.

'That's okay,' she said, 'If I don't sell more ass this month, I'm going to lose my damn car.'


A shepherd was herding his flock in a remote pasture when suddenly a brand new Jeep Cherokee advanced out of a dust cloud towards him.

The driver, a young blonde man in a Hugo Boss suit, Gucci shoes, Ray Ban sunglasses and a YSL tie leaned out of the window and said, 'If I can tell you exactly how many sheep you have in your flock, will you give me one?'

The shepherd looks at the yuppie, then at his peacefully grazing flock and calmly answers, 'Sure.'

The yuppie parks the car, whips out his laptop, connects it to a mobile phone, surfs to a NASA page on the internet where he calls up a GPS satellite navigation system, scans the area, opens up a database and 60 Excel spreadsheets with complex formulas. Finally he prints out a 150 page report on his hi-tech miniaturised printer, turns to the shepherd and says, 'You have here exactly 1586 sheep.'

'This is correct and as agreed you can take one of the sheep,' says the shepherd.

He watches the young man make a selection and bundle it in to his Cherokee.

Then he says, 'If I can tell you exactly what your business is, will you give me my property back?'

'Okay, why not,' answers the young man.

'You are a consultant,' says the shepherd.

'This is correct,' says the yuppie, 'How did you guess that?

'Easy,' answers the shepherd.

'You turn up here although nobody invited you, you want to be paid for an answer to a question I never asked, you gave me information I already knew and you don't know Jack-shit about my business because you took my dog'.

# BLONDE LOGIC

**A** single mum goes to the welfare office to register for child benefits.

'How many children?' asks the welfare officer.

'Ten,' she answers.

'Ten?' says the welfare officer. 'What are their names?'

'Craig, Craig, Craig, Craig, Craig, Craig, Craig, Craig, Craig and Craig'

'Doesn't that get confusing?'

'Nah!' says the chick 'It's great because if they are out playing in the street I just have to shout, "CRAAIG, YER DINNER'S READY" or, "CRAAIG, GO TO BED NOW," and they all do it . . .'

'What if you want to speak to one individually?' says the perturbed welfare officer.

'That's easy,' says the mum, 'I just use their surnames . . .'


**I**t's always puzzled me,' said the blonde looking up from the newspaper she was reading, 'How the Lord gets it right every time.'

'How's that?' says her husband.

'People always seem to die in alphabetical order.'


**O**ne blonde was explaining to the other how the Lord often compensates for a person's natural deficiencies.

'You see,' he said, 'If someone is a bit blind, he might have a very good sense of hearing or if his sense of taste has gone, he may have a keen sense of smell.'

'I agree with you,' said the other blonde. 'I've always noticed that if someone has one short leg, the other one is always just that little bit longer.'

Then there was the blonde terrorist who blew up a bus. She burned her lips on the exhaust pipe.

There was the blonde fisherman whose last wish was to be buried at sea, which was most unfortunate for his three friends, who died digging the grave . . .

A blonde rang the airport and asked, 'How long does it take to fly to London?'

'Just a minute, madam,' came the reply.

'Thanks,' said the blonde and put the phone down.

A blonde workman who fell 30 metres from a building site was asked if he was hurt by the fall.

'Indeed not,' he replied, 'It wasn't the fall that hurt me at all, it was the sudden stop.'

A passer-by watched two blonde workmen in a park. One was digging holes and the other was immediately filling them in again.

'Tell me,' said the passer-by, 'What on earth are you doing?'

'Well,' said the digger, 'Usually there are three of us. I dig, Tom plants the tree and Dick fills in the hole.

'Today Tom is off ill, but that doesn't mean Dick and I get the day off, does it?'

**A** blonde workman was digging a hole in a road when a passer-by asked him what he was going to do with all the soil.

'Ah, well,' he replied, 'I'll dig another hole.'

'But what if it doesn't all fit in?'

'Oh, I've thought of that,' said the blonde, 'I'll dig the next hole deeper.'

**T** wo blondes met in the street and one said to the other, 'Have you seen Jennifer lately, Pat?'

Pat said, 'Well, I have and I haven't.'

The friend asked, 'What do you mean by that?'

Pat said, 'It's like this, I saw a woman who I thought was Jennifer and she saw a lady that she thought was me. And when we got up to one another, it was neither of us.'

This young man who has been dating a blonde girl, comes home all excited to tell his mother he's fallen in love and going to get married.

He says, 'Just for fun, Ma, I'm going to bring over three women and you just try and guess which one I'm going to marry.'

The mother agrees.

The next day he brings along three beautiful blondes and sits them down on the couch and they chat away for a while.

After a while, he takes his mother into kitchen and says, 'Right, mother, can you guess which one I'm going to marry?'

She immediately replies, 'The one in the middle.'

'That's amazing, Mum. You're right. How did you know?'

'I don't like her.'


The young blonde wife thought she was a bit pregnant and it being the first time, she went to see the doctor, to see if all was right.

Coming home to her husband, she explained the doctor said he needed a sample.

Not wanting to seem ignorant of such things she had waited to ask her husband what 'a sample' was.

He did not know either.

So he said, 'Go see Mrs King, next door, she had 18 children, she is bound to know.'

So the young blonde wanders off to the widow's house.

She returns about ten minutes later, her dress all torn, he hair a shambles, her face all scratched.

Her husband asks, 'What happened to you?'

The blonde wife answers: 'Well I went to the widow and asked her what a sample was.

'Pee in a bottle,' she says to me.

'Shit in your hat,' I says to her.

'And the fight was on . . .'

Two blonde farmers were driving their tractor down the middle of a country road.

A car comes around the corner, backs hard to avoid them, skids, tumbles twice and lands in a field.

'It's just as well we got out of that field,' said one to the other.

Two blondes had just won $5,000,000 in a lottery.

They were having a pint in a pub. Tim says to Sam, 'What about all them begging letters.'

Sam replies, 'We'll just keep sending them.'

Two blondes were walking down a road one day.

'Can you see that beautiful wood over there?' said the first blonde.

Replied the second, 'Sorry, I can't see it; there are too many trees in the way!

On a drive in the country, a city slicker noticed a blonde farmer lifting a pig up to an apple tree and holding the pig there as it ate one apple after another.

'Maybe I don't know what I'm talking about,' said the city slicker, 'But if you just shook the tree so the apples fell to the ground, wouldn't it save a lot of time?'

'Time?' said the farmer. 'What does time matter to a pig?'

Old blonde Mrs Murphy went to the doctor.

'Doctor,' she says, 'I want to go on the Pill.'

'On the Pill, Mrs Murphy? But you're over 70! Haven't you heard of the menopause?'

'Of course I have,' she says, 'But my husband has got some of them Viagra tablets and he's a man o' pause no longer . . .'

**A** farmer sold his blonde neighbour a donkey.
Three weeks later, they met in the pub and the blonde neighbour says, 'Hey, that donkey you sold me went and died.'

The former owner just sipped his pint and replied, 'Gee, it never did that to me!'

**A** blonde went outside to check her mailbox and her neighbour kept an eye on her.

She had no mail, so she went back inside her house.

Two minutes later, the same blonde went outside for the second time to check her mailbox and still, she had no mail. The neighbour watched with interest.

One minute later, again the woman comes outside to check her mailbox for the third time and again, she had no mail.

This time, her neighbour went up to her and said, 'The mailman won't be here for another three hours, why do you keep on checking your mail?'

The blonde said, 'Oh, because my computer keeps on saying, "You've got mail".'

**A** blonde walks into a hairdresser's, wearing headphones. She says to the hairdresser, 'Please cut my hair, but, whatever you do, don't knock the headphones off!'

Alas, during the cutting, the hairdresser slips and the headphones accidentally fall off.

The blonde falls over dead.

The shocked hairdresser picks up the headphones and listens.

The taped voice is saying, 'Breathe in, breathe out, breathe in, breathe out . . .'

**B**e sure you lock your doors and windows at home. A local blonde man was murdered in his home over the weekend.

Detectives found him face down in the bathtub.

The tub had been filled with milk and cornflakes and a banana was sticking out of his ass.

Police suspect a cereal killer.

# ON THE ISLAND

Three blondes are stranded on an island.
A good fairy appears and says that she will grant each person a wish.

The first blonde says that she wants to get home and needs to escape the island.

She asks for a cell phone and calls the Army for help.

The second blonde says that she also wants to escape and asks for a flare which she sets off.

The third blonde wishes that she be even smarter than her two friends.

The fairy waves her wand, changes her hair colour to black and she says, 'Let's go home over the bridge.'

A blonde, a brunette and a redhead are walking along their island beach when one sees a bottle lying on the ground.

It turns out there's a genie and as there are three wishes they get one each. The brunette goes first and says, 'I miss my family; I wish I was home again.'

Poof! The brunette disappears.

The redhead takes her turn. She too wishes to be returned to her ancestral home. Her wish is granted.

There the blonde stands, all alone on the beach.

She starts to cry and says, 'I wish my two friends would come back . . .'

# BLONDE PARTNERS

Two blonde neighbours are chatting over a cup of tea when Jan glances out the window and shrieks, 'Oh no, here comes my Johnny up the front walk with a bouquet of flowers!

'I suppose this means I'll be spending the entire weekend on my back with my legs in the air!'

In a puzzled tone, her friend Sue replies, 'What's the matter, don't you have a vase?'

Two blondes are chatting over the back fence.
Jan says, 'I'm so sorry to hear about your Tommy passing away. What was it that he died of?'

Sue looks around and replies quietly, 'Oh, he died of the gonorrhoea.'

In a suspicious tone Jan says, 'I thought I read he died of the diarrhoea?'

Again Sue looks around and then exclaims, 'Well, actually he did, but I want the world to remember him as a real man, instead of the dribbling little shit that he was!'

Bernie was a member of a Toast Masters' Club.
One evening at the meeting, a contest was held to see who could deliver the best toast.

Bernie won the contest with the following verse, 'Here's to the best years o' me life, spent between the legs of me wife.'

When he arrived home, his beautiful blonde wife asked him how the Toast Masters' meeting went and he said, 'I won the contest for the best toast of the evening.'

His wife then asked what his toast was and he said, 'My toast was, 'Here's to the best years o' me life, spent in Church with my wife'.'

His wife said, 'Why, Bernie, that's so nice of you to include me in your toast.'

The next morning, she was downtown shopping and ran into the local policeman who had also been at the Toast Masters' meeting with her husband.

He said, 'Well, well, well, that was some great toast that your husband gave at the Toast Masters' meeting last evening. He won first prize.'

'Yes, that's what he told me,' said the wife, 'but he wasn't quite honest with the facts. He's only been there twice, the first time he fell asleep and the second I had to pull him by the ears to make him come . . .!'

His blonde wife had been killed in an accident and the police were questioning the husband.

'Did she say anything before she died?' asked the sergeant.

'She spoke without interruption for about 40 years,' came the reply.

A heavily pregnant blonde girl phones the maternity hospital, obviously in some state of agitation.

'Nurse, nurse, I think my waters have broken.'

'Okay love, stay calm love,' said the nurse. 'Where are you ringing from?'

'Oh, from my vee to my knees . . .'

# BLONDE RIDDLES

**Q.** How many blondes does it take to make chocolate chip cookies?

**A.** *Seven. One to make the dough and six to peel the M&Ms.*

**Q.** Why can't blondes make Kool Aid?

**A.** *Because they can't figure out how to get eight cups of water into that tiny little package.*

**Q.** What do you call a blonde that has one leg shorter than the other?

**A.** *Eileen.*

**Q.** How can you tell if a blonde is having a bad day?

**A.** *Her tampon is in her ear and she can't find her pen!*

**Q.** How many blondes does it take to milk a cow?

**A.** *Eleven. One to hold the udders and ten to lift the cow up and down.*

**Q.** Why did the blonde have lipstick on her steering wheel?

**A.** *She was trying to blow the horn.*

**Q.** What is the quickest way to get into a blonde's pants?

**A.** *Pick them up off the floor.*

**Q.** Why don't blondes play Frisbee?
**A.** *It hurts their teeth.*

**Q.** What do you call a blonde with half a brain?
**A** *Gifted!*

**Q.** How do blonde brain-cells die?
**A.** *Alone.*

**Q.** How can you tell if a blonde has been using the computer?
**A.** *The joystick is wet.*

**Q.** What happened to the blonde tap dancer?
**A.** *She slipped off and fell in the sink.*

**Q.** Why are blonde jokes so short?
**A.** *So brunettes can remember them.*

**Q.** What do you do if a blonde throws a grenade at you?
**A.** *You pick it up, pull the pin and throw it back.*

**Q.** How can you confuse a blonde?
**A.** *Put her in a round room and tell her to sit in the corner.*

**Q.** What do you call a smart blonde?
**A.** *A Golden Retriever!*

**Q.** A blond and a brunette jump off the Empire State Building. It takes the blonde three minutes longer to hit the ground than it does the brunette. Why?
**A.** *Because she had to stop to ask for directions.*

**Q.** Santa Claus, the Easter Bunny, the Tooth Fairy and a blonde are walking down the street when they spot $100 on the ground. Who gets the money?

**A.** *None. Santa Claus, the Easter Bunny and the tooth fairy do not exist and the blonde thought it was a lolly wrapper.*

**Q.** Why do blondes take the pill?

**A.** *So they know which day of the week it is.*

**Q.** What is a blonde's idea of safe sex??

**A.** *Lock the car doors.*

**Q.** Why don't blondes eat bananas?

**A.** *They can't find the zipper.*

**Q.** How did the blonde try to kill the fish?

**A.** *She tried to drown it.*

**Q.** What's the difference between a blonde and a 747?
**A.** *Not everyone has been in a 747.*

**Q.** What do you do if a bird shits on your car?
**A.** *You never take her out again.*

**Q.** What nursery rhyme do blondes know meticulously off by heart?
**A.** *'Hump-me, dump-me . . .'*

**Q.** How do you brainwash a blonde?
**A.** *Give her a douche and shake her upside down.*

**Q.** Did you hear about the figure-conscious blonde who had square boobs?
**A.** *She forgot to take the tissues out of the box.*

**Q.** What do you call a fly buzzing around in a blonde's brain?
**A.** *A space invader.*

**Q.** Why does it take longer to build a blonde snowman?
**A.** *You have to hollow out its head first.*

**Q.** Why did the blonde throw her clock out the window?
**A.** *So she could see time fly!*

**Q.** Why couldn't the blonde add 10 and 7 on a calculator?
**A.** *She couldn't find the 10 key.*

**Q.** Why did the blonde girl take a ladder to the bar?
**A.** *Because she heard that the drinks were on the house.*

**Q.** What do you call a blonde with a brain?
**A.** *Pregnant.*

**Q.** What do you call a dead blonde in the closet?
**A.** *Last year's Hide and Seek Champion!*

**Q.** How do you get a one armed blonde that is hanging on for dear life out of a tree?
**A.** *Wave.*

**Q.** How can you tell if a blonde has used a computer?
**A.** *There's white-out on the screen.*

**Q.** Why did it take the blonde so long to save someone's life?
**A.** *She had to ask someone what number to call for 911.*

**Q.** What would a blonde do with a brain if she had one?
**A.** *Save it for later!*

# BLONDE SPORTSMEN AND WOMEN

Two bowling teams, one all blonde and one all brunette, charter a double-decker bus for a weekend bowling tournament in London.

The brunette team rides in the bottom of the bus.

The blonde team rides on the top level.

The brunette team down below is having a great time, when one of them realises she hasn't heard anything from the blondes upstairs.

She decides to go up and investigate.

When the brunette reaches the top, she finds all the blondes frozen in fear, staring straight ahead at the road and clutching the seats in front of them with white knuckles.

She says, 'What the heck's going' on up here? We're having a fantastic time downstairs!'

One of the blondes looks up and says, 'Yeah, but you've got a driver!'

A blonde is out playing golf one sunny day, when she suddenly screams and runs back to the club house.

She approaches the resident pro and tells him, 'I've just been stung by a bee!'

'Where were you stung?' asks the pro.

'Between the first and second holes.' she replies.

'I'm not surprised,' answers the pro. 'Your stance is far too wide.'

**T**wo blonde duck-shooters were out shooting ducks.

One took aim and hit a bird which tumbled out of the sky to land at his feet.

'You should have saved the bullet,' said the other. 'The fall would have killed him, anyway . . .'

**T**wo blondes were out duck-shooting.

They had their guns and dogs and walked for hours with no success.

Dropping into the pub on the way back they listened with envy to all the other hunters who had obviously been very successful.

'Where do you think we went wrong?' asked one.

His friend thought for a minute.

'You know, I think it must be that we're not throwing the dogs high enough.'

**T**wo blonde golfers are teeing off on a foggy day on a par three.

They can see the flag, but not the green.

The first golfer hits his ball into the fog and the second golfer does the same.

They proceed to the green to find their balls.

One ball is about two metres from the cup while the other found its way into the cup for a hole-in-one.

Both were playing the same type of balls, Top-Flite 2, so they couldn't determine which ball was which.

They decide to ask the course pro to decide their fate.

After congratulating both golfers on their fine shots, the golf pro asks, 'Now, which one of you is playing the orange ball . . .?'

**A** young blonde man was visiting his cousin.
While there he decided to do a bit of fishing.

As he sat there on the pier, his cousin walked by.

'What are you doing?' asked Pete.

'Fishing,' said Mac.

'Caught anything?'

'Not a bite.'

'What are you using for bait?'

'Worms.'

'Let me see.'

The young blonde man lifted the line from the water and handed it to his cousin.

The cousin took a flask of whisky and dipped the worm in it.

He handed it back to his cousin who cast his line once more.

As soon as the worm hit the water, his rod bent over double and the line ran out.

'Have you got a bite?'

'No!' shouted the blonde, fighting with the rod, 'The worm's got a salmon by the throat!'


**'A** nyone who can guess how many ducks I have in this sack can have both of them,' said the blonde bloke.

'Three,' replied another blonde.

'That's near enough,' said the first.


**A** blonde was fishing and it started to rain, so he moved under the bridge for shelter.

His mate saw him and called, 'Sam, are you afraid of the rain?'

Sam replied, 'No . . . the fish come here for shelter.'

**A** blonde went fishing one day.

He looked over the side of his boat and saw a snake with a frog in its mouth.

Feeling sorry for the frog, he reached down, gently took the frog from the snake and set the frog free.

But then he felt sorry for the snake.

He looked around the boat, but he had no food.

All he had was a bottle of bourbon.

So he opened the bottle and gave the snake a few shots.

The snake went off happy, the frog was happy and the man was happy to have performed such good deeds.

He thought everything was great until about ten minutes passed and he heard something knock against the side of the boat.

In stunned disbelief, the fisherman looked down and saw the snake was back with two other frogs!

**W**hile out one morning in the park, a jogger found a brand new tennis ball and, seeing no-one around that it might belong to, he slipped it into the pocket of his shorts.

Later, on his way home, he stopped at the pedestrian crossing, waiting for the lights to change.

A blonde girl standing next to him eyed the large bulge in his shorts. 'What's that?' she asked, her eyes gleaming with lust.

'Tennis ball,' came the breathless reply.

'Oh,' said the blonde girl sympathetically, 'That must be painful. I had tennis elbow once.'


**T**here were two blondes out hunting.

It started getting dark and they realised that they were lost.

One of the blondes said to the other that she had heard that if you ever get lost in the bush, to shoot three shots into the air and sit down and wait for someone to find you.

So they did.

After a few hours went by and no one had come they decided to shoot three more shots in the air.

It was late now and no one had come, they were going to shoot some more shots when one of blondes said, 'Someone better hurry up and save us, we only have two more arrows left . . .'


**A** blonde arrived for her first golf lesson and the pro asked her to take a swing at a ball to see how well she'd do.

The blonde did so and completely stuffed the shot.

The pro said, 'Your swing is good but you're gripping the club too hard. Grip the club gently as you would your husband's penis.'

The blonde took another shot and nailed the ball 350 metres straight down the fairway.

The pro said, 'That was excellent! Let's try it again, only this time, take the club out of your mouth . . .'

**H**eard the one about the three blondes who went ice fishing and didn't catch anything?

By the time they cut a hole big enough for the boat to fit in it was time to go home.


**T**hree blondes are sitting by the side of a river holding fishing poles with the lines in the water.

A Game Warden comes up behind them, taps them on the shoulder and says, 'Excuse me, ladies, I'd like to see your fishing licences.'

'We don't have any,' replies the first blonde.

'Well, if you're going to fish, you need fishing licences,' says the Warden.

'But officer,' replies the second blonde, 'We aren't fishing. All we have are magnets at the end of our lines and we're collecting debris off the bottom of the river.'

The Warden lifts up all the lines and, sure enough, there are horseshoe magnets tied on the end of each line.

'Well, I know of no law against it,' says the Warden, 'Take all the debris you want.'

And with that, the Warden left.

As soon as the Game Warden was out of sight, the three blondes started laughing hysterically.

'What a dumb Fish Cop,' the second blonde says to the other two, 'Doesn't he know that there are steelhead in this river?'


**A** guy took his blonde girlfriend to an American football game for the first time.

After the game he asked his girlfriend how she liked the game.

'Oh, I really liked it,' she said, 'but I just couldn't understand why they were killing each other for 25 cents.'

'What on earth do you mean?'

'Well I saw them flip a coin and one team got it and then for the rest of the game all they kept screaming was, "Get the quarter back! Get the quarter back!".'

Two blonde hunters were dragging a deer back to their truck when another hunter happened by.

'I don't want to tell you what to do,' he said, 'But it's easier if you drag the deer the other way so the antlers don't dig into the ground.'

After the hunter left, the two decided to try it his way.

After a while, one said to the other, 'Man that guy was right. This is easier.'

'Yeah,' the other replied, 'But we keep getting further and further away from the truck.'

There was a blonde who was at an all-blonde football match. At halftime he was called down to answer questions to see if he could win $1000.

The first question was what is 10 plus 11?

He hesitates and says, 'Hmm, 5!'

The host says, 'No I'm sorry, that's incorrect.'

All of the blondes in the stadium chanted, 'Give him another chance, give him another chance!'

So the host agrees and said, 'Okay, how about 5 plus 5.'

He answers and says 20.

Again all the blondes chanted, 'Give him another chance, give him another chance.'

So the host agrees again and says, 'Okay, last chance, what is 2 plus 2?'

The blonde says 4!

And the blonde audience says, 'Give him another chance, give him another chance!'

# I WISH,
# I WISH...

**A** blonde drunk was staggering home with a bottle of whisky in his back pocket when he slipped and fell heavily.

Struggling to his feet, he felt something wet running down his leg.

'Please, God,' he implored, 'let it be blood!'

**A** blonde youth was walking home one night when, lo and behold, he saw a leprechaun.

He snuck up and caught him, then demanded three wishes for the little man's freedom.

'Granted,' said the man in green, 'But whatever I do for you, your main rival will get twofold!'

The blonde man agreed.

'For my first wish I'd like a mansion full of expensive antiques and beautiful women.'

'Granted and of course your rival gets two!'

'For my second wish I'd like the most expensive car in the world.'

'Granted and of course your rival gets two of them.'

Now by this stage the man was getting distressed about his hated rival getting twice as much as he was.

Suddenly inspiration hits the blonde youth.

'For my third wish, I want you to remove one of my testicles!'

# BLONDES AND ANIMALS

Two blonde blokes walk into a pet shop.
They go over to the bird section.

One says to the other, 'That's them!'

The clerk comes over and asks if he can help them.

'Yeah, we'll take four of them birds in that cage up there. Put them into a paper bag.'

The clerk does so and the two guys pay for the birds and leave the shop.

They get into a van and drive until they are high up in the hills and stop at the top of a cliff with a 500 foot drop.

'This looks like a grand place, eh?' says the first blonde.

'Oh, yeah, this looks good,' replies the second.

They flip a coin and the first blonde gets to go first.

He then takes two birds out of the bag, places them on his shoulders and jumps off the cliff.

The second blonde watches as his mate drops off the edge and goes straight down for a few seconds, followed by a dreadful SPLAT.

He looks over the edge of the cliff, shakes his head and says, 'Blow that, this budgie jumping is too dangerous for me!'

There once was a blonde who had two horses.
She couldn't tell her two horses apart so she decided to ask her neighbour to help her out.

She said to her neighbour, 'I have two horses that I can't tell apart, can you help me?'

'Sure,' said her neighbour, 'Maybe you should nick the ears of one and then you could tell them apart.'

So the blonde went home and did that. The next day the blonde went to check up on her horses.

However she still could not tell them apart, because the other horse also had nicked ears. She went back over to her neighbour's.

'My other horse has nicked ears, too.' she said, 'Do you have any other ideas as to how to tell them apart? They are both girls.'

'Hmm.' said her neighbour,' Cut one's tail shorter than the other!'

So the blonde went home and did that. The next day, though, when she looked at them, both horses had the same length of tail!

As a last resort the neighbour suggested that she should consider measuring the horses. Maybe one stands taller than the other one.

The blonde did this and excitedly rushed home and phoned her neighbour. 'You were right!' she said, 'The black horse is bigger than the white one!'

A bloke walks into a pub with a crocodile on a leash and puts it up on the bar.

He turns to the amazed drinkers, 'Here's the deal. I'll open this crocodile's mouth and place my dick inside. Then the croc will close his mouth for one minute. He'll then open his mouth and I'll remove my wedding tackle unscathed. In return for witnessing this spectacle, each of you will buy me a drink.'

After a few moments' silence the crowd murmurs approval.

The man stands up on the bar, drops his trousers and places his dick in the crocodile's mouth.

The croc closes his mouth as the crowd gasps. After a minute, the man grabs a beer bottle and whacks the crocodile hard on the top of its head.

The croc opens his mouth and the man removes his genitals—unscathed as promised.

The crowd cheers and the first of his free drinks is delivered.

The man calls for silence and makes another offer. 'I'll pay anyone $1000 who's willing to give it a try.'

A hush falls over the crowd. No-one is game.

Then after a while, a hand goes up at the back.

It's a blonde.

'I'll try,' she says. 'But only if you promise not to hit me on the head with the beer bottle . . .'


This blonde decides to try horseback riding, for the first time.

She mounts the horse unassisted and it springs into motion. It gallops at a steady pace, but the blonde begins to slip from the saddle. In terror, she grabs for the horse's mane, but cannot get a firm grip.

She throws her arms around the horse's neck, but slides down the side, while it gallops on.

The blonde tries to leap from the horse to safety. But her foot becomes entangled in the stirrup and she is now in all sorts of trouble, with her head repeatedly banging against the ground as the horse continues its gallop.

The blonde starts to lose consciousness.

But luckily, one of the checkout girls sees her predicament, rushes over and unplugs the horse . . .

A little girl was talking to her teacher about whales. The teacher said it was physically impossible for a whale to swallow a human because even though they were a very large mammal their throat was very small.

The little girl stated that Jonah was swallowed by a whale.

The teacher reiterated that a whale could not swallow a human; it was impossible.

The little girl said, 'When I get to heaven I will ask Jonah.'

The teacher asked, 'What if Jonah went to hell?'

The little girl replied, 'Then you ask him.'

A barracuda swims into Poseidon's Bar & Grill and orders a glass of clam juice.

When the bar tender returns the barracuda asks if he would like to hear a blonde joke.

The bar tender leans over the bar and says, 'Before you do I will warn you, pal! Over there at the end of the bar is King Neptune's ex-captain of the guards who was fired today. He is blonde. At the other end of the bar is a professional killer shark, he is blonde. My 250 kilogram doorman is in a bad mood because a whale swallowed his wife three days ago, she was blonde. And I lost my scalp to a sword fish three weeks ago, I was also blonde. So, do you still want to tell your joke?'

The barracuda looks at his watch and replies, 'I'd like to share a joke with you guys, but unfortunately I have to leave here in three hours and don't have the time to explain it to all you blondes.'

# BLONDES AND BARS

**T**hree men are in a bar having a drink when a great-looking, blonde comes up to them, wiggles her boobs, bats her eyes and says, 'Whoever can say "liver" and "cheese" in a sentence can have me.'

So the first bloke says, 'I love liver and cheese.'

The blonde replies, 'That's not good enough.'

The second bloke says, 'I hate liver and cheese.'

She says, 'That's not creative enough.'

Finally, the third bloke says, 'Liver alone . . . cheese mine.'

## WHY BEER IS BETTER THAN BLONDES

- You can enjoy a beer all month long.
- You don't have to wine and dine beer.
- Your beer will always wait patiently for you in the car while you play footy.
- When your beer goes flat, you toss it out.
- Hangovers go away.
- A beer label comes off without a fight.
- Beer is never late.
- Beer doesn't get jealous when you grab another beer.
- When you go to a bar, you know you can always pick up a beer.
- Beer never gets a headache.
- Beer stains wash out.

- After you've had a beer, the bottle is still worth 5 cents.
- A beer won't get upset if you come home and have another beer.
- If you pour a beer right, you'll always get good head.
- A beer always goes down easy.
- You can have more than one beer a night and not feel guilty.
- You can share a beer with your friends.
- You always know you're the first one to pop a beer.
- Beer is always wet.
- Beer doesn't demand equality.
- You can have a beer in public.
- A beer doesn't care when you come.
- A frigid beer is a good beer.
- You don't have to wash a beer before it tastes good.
- If you change beers you don't have to pay alimony.

The blonde lodger came in blind drunk one night. The next morning he staggered down to breakfast.

The landlady looked at him, then said in a haughty voice, 'So, how do you find yourself this morning?'

'Same as yesterday,' the blonde replied. 'I just threw back the sheets and there I was . . .'

A string walks into a bar and says to the blonde bartender, 'Hi, can I have a vodka, please?'

The bartender says, 'Sorry, we don't serve strings around here.'

The string leaves and goes around the corner, ties himself in a knot and ruffles his top and bottom.

He goes up to the bartender and again asks for vodka and the bartender says, 'Aren't you the string that just came in here?'

The string replies, 'No, I'm afraid not!'

(A frayed knot . . .)

Two blonde guys were sitting in the corner of a newly refurbished bar.

Across the wall opposite was a huge mirror, five metres long and stretching from floor to ceiling.

Glancing around the room, blonde number one suddenly spotted their reflection in the mirror.

He whispered. 'Don't look now, but there's two blokes over there that are the spitting image of us!'

'Yes!' said the other, spotting the reflection. 'They're wearing identical clothes and everything!'

'That does it,' said the first blonde. 'I'm going to buy them a drink.'

But as he started to rise from his seat and take a step, the other said, 'Quick, sit down, one of them's coming over!'

An infamous blonde stud with a long list of conquests walked into his neighbourhood bar and ordered a drink. The bartender thought he looked worried and asked him if anything was wrong.

'I'm scared out of my mind,' the stud replied. 'Some pissed-off husband wrote to me and said he'd kill me if I didn't stop sleeping with his wife.'

'So stop,' the barkeep said.

'I can't,' the womaniser replied, taking a long swill. 'The prick didn't sign his name!'

A slimy fellow proposed a one dollar bar bet to a well endowed young blonde lady that despite her dress being buttoned to the neck, he could touch her breasts without touching her clothes.

Since this didn't seem remotely possible, she was intrigued and accepted the bet.

He stepped up, cupped his hands around her breasts and squeezed firmly.

With a baffled look, she said, 'Hey, you touched my clothes.'

And he replied, 'Damn. I owe you a dollar . . .'

A blonde pirate with a peg leg, a hook and an eye-patch walks into a bar.

The bartender says, 'Where did you get that peg leg?'

The pirate replies, 'We were swimming one day, on the high seas, when a big shark came up and bit off me leg.'

The bartender asks, 'Well, where did you get the hook, then?'

The pirate responds, 'We were in a battle with Capt'n Bloodeye and my hand was cut off at the bone.'

The bartender asks, 'Then where did ya get the eye-patch?'

The pirate says, 'One day, I looked up at a gull flying overhead and it pooped right in me eye.'

The puzzled bartender says, 'Why would you need an eye-patch after that?'

The blonde pirate replies, 'First day with the hook . . .'

A drunk blonde is in a bar, lying on the floor and looking the worse for wear.

Other hotel patrons decide to be good Samaritans and to take him home.

They pick him up off the floor and drag him out the door.

On the way to the car, he falls down three times.

When they get to his house, they help him out of the car and he falls down four more times.

Mission accomplished, they prop him against the door jam and ring the doorbell.

'Here's your husband!' they exclaim proudly.

'Where is his wheelchair?' asks the puzzled wife.

A blonde business man walks into his club bar and is surprised to find he's the only customer.

He asks for a beer, but the barman says, 'I'll just be a few minutes sir, I've got to change the barrel—help yourself to the savoury snacks.'

So the man is sitting quietly nibbling the nibbles, when he hears a voice, 'I tell you what mate, you're looking really good tonight, that suit is really you.'

He looks around, but he's still alone.

Then he hears '. . . and that new haircut, it couldn't be better.'

Again he looks around. Nothing.

'. . . and have you lost weight. I don't think I've ever seen you looking so well'

Still no-one about.

After a while the barman returns and the man says, 'You won't believe what's happened. I was just sitting here on my own and I heard this voice say I look great, my suit is really me and that I've never looked so well. And yet there's no-one here.'

'Oh' said the barman, 'That'll be the nuts. They're complimentary . . .'

Two fat blondes are sitting in a pub. One says to the other, 'Your round.'

And the other replies, 'So are you, ya fat bastard!'

A blonde tradey, who was obviously the victim of a nasty accident, came staggering into the pub with both arms in plaster casts.

'I'll have a beer, thanks mate,' he said to the barman. 'And could you hold it up to my lips for me?'

'No worries,' said the barman.

'Couldn't light a fag for me, too, could you?' asked the bloke.

'Not a problem,' said the barman.

'Thanks, mate,' said the bloke. 'Me wallet's in me back pocket, if you'd like to get it out for me.'

'There you go,' said the barman.

'Cheers,' said the bloke. 'By the way, where's the toilet?'

And without a moment's hesitation, the barman said, 'Go two blocks up the street, turn right and it's the second on the left.'

Chad went to a bar and ordered a drink. A few minutes later, a beautiful blonde sat down next to him and started coming on to him. After a little while, she invited him back to her place.

Overcome with excitement, Chad agreed.

When they got to the bedroom, Chad exclaimed 'Wow! A waterbed. I've never had sex on a waterbed before.'

Soon they were both naked and going at it.

The blonde stopped him and said, 'Before we go any further, don't you think you should put on some protection?'

'Good idea,' he responded and got up.

Chad walked out of the room and when he came back, he was wearing a life preserver.

# BLONDES AND MARRIAGE

Three women are having lunch, discussing their husbands. The first says, 'My husband is cheating on me, I just know it. I found a pair of stockings in his jacket pocket and they weren't mine!'

The second says, 'My husband is cheating on me, I just know it. I found a condom in his wallet, so I poked it full of holes with my sewing needle!'

The third woman fainted.

I bought my beautiful blonde wife a mood ring so that I could tell when she was in a good mood for me to ask if I could go fishing.

When she is in a good mood, the ring is a pretty light green that matches the colour of her eyes.

When she's not, the ring leaves a little red mark right in the middle of my forehead.

James tells his pretty blonde mother how much fun he and his father had when she was away on a business trip.

'Everyday Aunt Miriam visited us and brought candy for me,' said the boy.

'Daddy entertained her with wine and then they did the same thing you and Uncle Nick do when Dad is out of town.'

**T**his blonde decides one day to surprise her husband by painting a couple of rooms of their house while he is at work.

As soon as he leaves for work she begins painting furiously.

At 5.30 he arrives home to the distinctive smell of paint.

He walks into the living room and finds his wife lying on the floor in a pool of sweat.

He notices that she is not only wearing a ski jacket but also her fur coat.

'Honey, are you okay?' he asks her.

'Yes,' she replies.

'Then what are you doing?' he asks.

'I wanted to surprise you by painting the house,' she replies.

'Then why are you wearing a ski jacket over a fur coat?' he asks.

'Well,' she replies 'I was reading the directions on the paint can and it said "FOR BEST RESULTS, PUT ON TWO COATS".'

## REPAID DEBTS

A guy goes over to his friend's house, rings the bell and the blonde wife answers.

'Hi, is Tony home?' says the visitor.

'No, he went to the store,' says the blonde wife.

'Well, you mind if I wait?'

'No, come in.'

They sit down and the friend says, 'You know, Nora, you have the greatest breasts I have ever seen. I'd give you 100 bucks if I could just see one.'

Nora thinks about this for a second and figures what the hell—100 bucks. She opens her robe and shows one.

He promptly thanks her and throws a hundred bucks on the table.

They sit there a while longer and the blonde bloke says, 'They are so beautiful I've got to see the both of them. I'll give you another 100 bucks if I could just see the both of them together.'

Nora thinks about this and thinks what the hell, opens her robe and gives him a nice long look of both her voluptuous breasts.

The visitor thanks her, throws another hundred bucks on the table and then says he can't wait any longer and leaves.

A while later the husband arrives home and his wife says, 'You know, your weird friend came over.'

The husband thinks about this for a second and says, 'Oh yeah? Did he drop off the 200 bucks he owes me?'

# A DICTIONARY FOR BLONDE PARENTS

**A**mnesia
A condition that enables a woman who has gone through labour to ever have sex again.

**B**ottle feeding
An opportunity for Daddy to get up at 2 am too.

**D**efence
What you'd better have around the yard if you're going to let the children play outside.

**D**rooling
How teething babies wash their chins.

**D**umb waiter
One who asks if the kids would care to order dessert.

**F**amily planning
The art of spacing your children the proper distance apart to keep you from falling into financial disaster.

**F**eed back
The inevitable result when a baby doesn't appreciate the strained carrots.

**F**ull name
What you call your child when you're mad at him.

**G**randparents
The people who think your children are wonderful even though they're sure you're not raising them right.

**H**earsay
What toddlers do when anyone mutters a dirty word.

**I**mpregnable
A woman whose memory of labour is still vivid.

**I**ndependent
How we want our children to be as long as they do everything we say.

**L**ook out!
What it's too late for your child to do by the time you scream it.

**P**renatal
When your life was still somewhat your own.

**P**repared childbirth
A contradiction in terms.

**P**uddle
A small body of water that draws other small bodies wearing dry shoes.

**S**how off
A child who is more talented than yours.

**S**terilise
What you do to your first baby's pacifier by boiling it and to your last baby's pacifier by blowing on it.

**S**toreroom
The distance required between the supermarket aisles so that children in shopping carts can't quite reach anything.

**T**emper tantrums
What you should keep to a minimum so as to not upset the children.

**T**hunderstorm
A chance to see how many family members can fit into one bed.

**T**op bunk
Where you should never put a child wearing Superman PJs.

**T**wo minute warning
When the baby's face turns red and she begins to make those familiar grunting noises.

**V**erbal
Able to whine in words.

**W**eaker sex
The kind you have after the kids have worn you out.

**W**hodunit
One of the kids that lives in your house.

**W**hoops
An exclamation that translates roughly into 'get a sponge'.

## MY LEGS ARE KILLING ME

**T**wo blokes were out walking home from work one afternoon.

'Shit,' said the blonde bloke, 'As soon as I get home, I'm gonna rip the wife's knickers off!'

'What's the rush?' his mate asked.

'The bloody elastic in the legs is killing me . . .'

## OPPOSITES

'You and your husband don't seem to have an awful lot in common,' said the new tenant's neighbour. 'Why on earth did you get married?'

'I suppose it was the old business of "opposites attract",' was the reply. 'He wasn't pregnant and I was.'

## SILENT PARTNER

Matt's dad picked him up from school to take him to a dental appointment.

Knowing the parts for the school play were supposed to be posted today, he asked his son if he got a part.

Matt enthusiastically announced that he'd gotten a part. 'I play a man who's been married to his blonde wife for 20 years.'

'That's great, son. Keep up the good work and before you know it they'll be giving you a speaking part.'

## COMMUNICATION

A husband is about to leave on a business trip, 'Honey, if my business requires me to stay longer in that town, I'll send you a telegram.'

'Don't bother, dear. I read it already—it's in the pocket of your coat.'

When the young couple married, the wife put a wooden box under the marital bed and warned her husband not to ever open it until she was dead.

Time passed and although the husband was sometimes curious, he never broke trust and looked in the box.

After a period of 20 years the wife became unwell and had to spend an amount of time in hospital having her gall bladder removed.

The husband found the evenings long and uneventful in his wife's absence and one night opened the wooden box.

Inside he found three eggs and $25,000 in notes.

He returned them to the box, but when he wife returned from hospital, he asked her to explain.

'What are the eggs for?' he asked.

'Every time I have been unfaithful to you and our marriage I put an egg in the box.'

After thinking for a bit, the man reasoned that three instances of betrayal in 20 years wasn't too bad in this day and age.

'And what about the $25,000?' he asked.

The wife replied, 'Every time I got a dozen I sold them.'

## HOLIDAYS

Three men are arguing about when exactly does life begin? The first one says, 'At the time of conception.'

'At the time of birth,' argues the next.

'Oh, no,' says the third. 'Life begins when the wife takes the children and they all leave for vacation.'

A father was explaining the facts of life to his son. He covered the basic biology and then he moved on to the finer points of love-making.

F: All women are different son. One thing to keep in mind is that different women say different things during the act, even if you are doing the same thing.

S: What do you mean, Dad?

F: Their words will vary according to their occupation. For example, a prostitute will tend to say, 'Are you done yet?'

On the other hand, a nymphomaniac will ask, 'Are you done already?' A school teacher will say, "We are going to do this over and over again until you get it right!" A nurse will say, "This won't hurt one bit." Alternatively, a nurse may also say, "Pull down your pants and bend over." A bank teller will say, "Substantial penalty for early withdrawal." A stewardess will say, "Place this over your mouth and nose and breathe normally." A blonde will say, "That was fun—whatever it was."

S: And what does mother say?

F: She says, "Beige . . . beige . . . I think we should paint the ceiling beige".'

A market researcher called at a house and his knock was answered by a young blonde woman with three small children running around her.

He asked her if she minded replying to his questions.

She agreed, so he asked her if she knew his company, Ponds.

When she answered no, he mentioned that among their many products was Vaseline.

She certainly knew of that product.

When asked if she used it, the answer was 'Yes.'

Asked how she used it, she said, 'To assist sexual intercourse.'

The interviewer was amazed.

He said, 'I always ask that question because everyone uses our product and they always say they use it for the child's bicycle chain or the gate hinge; but I know that most use it for sexual intercourse. Since you've been so frank, could you tell me exactly how you use it?'

'Yes,' she said, 'We put it on the doorknob to keep the kids out.'

There was a boy who wasn't developing very well in his 'down-stairs department'.

So his blonde mum took him to the doctor to get him examined and see if there was anything the doctor could do.

'Well there isn't much wrong,' said the doctor, 'But if you feed him lots of toast, it should soon rectify itself.'

The next day, the boy comes home from school and there is a massive pile of toast on the table—about 30 pieces high.

'Aw, mum, is that all for me?' said the boy.

'No, son, the top two slices are for you—the rest is for your dad!'

After their baby was born, the panicked father went to see the obstetrician.

'Doctor,' the man said, 'I don't mind telling you, I'm a little upset because my daughter has red hair. She can't possibly be mine.'

'Nonsense,' the doctor said. 'Even though you have black hair and your wife is blonde, one of your ancestors may have contributed red hair to the gene pool.'

'It isn't possible,' the man insisted. 'This can't be, our families on my side has had jet-black hair for generations and on hers, it has always been blonde.'

'Well,' said the doctor, 'Let me ask you this. How often do you have sex?'

The man seemed a bit ashamed.

'I've been working very hard for the past year,' he replied carefully. 'We only made love once or twice every few months.'

'Well, there you have it!' the doctor said confidently. 'It's rust!'

A Welshman, a Scot and an Irishman are sitting in a pub a couple of days after Christmas.

The Welshman asks, 'What did you give your wife for Christmas?'

The Scot replies, 'A diamond ring and a pair of gloves.'

'Why the gloves?' asks Taffy.

'Well, if she doesn't like the ring, she can wear the gloves to cover it,' he replied.

'I got mine a necklace and a polo-neck sweater,' Taffy replied. 'If she doesn't like the necklace, she can wear the polo-neck sweater to cover it.'

'Perfectly logical,' agrees the Scot.

They then ask of the Irishman, 'What did you buy your wife for Christmas?'

The Irishman replied, 'I got my lovely blonde wife a handbag and a vibrator.'

'That's an odd combination, why those two items?' says Taffy.

'Well, if she doesn't like the handbag, she can go screw herself!'


A fter the party, as the couple was driving home, the woman asks her blonde husband, 'Honey, has anyone ever told you how handsome, sexy and irresistible to women you are?'

The flattered husband said, 'No, dear they haven't.'

The wife yells, 'Then what the heck gave you THAT idea!'


M arriage is the price men pay for sex. Sex is the price women pay for marriage.

## WRONG PERSON

A blonde woman was in the grocery store with a three-year-old girl in her basket.

As they passed the cookie section, the little girl asked for cookies and her mother told her, 'No.'

The little girl immediately began to whine and fuss and the mother said quietly, 'Now Mary, we just have half of the aisles left to go through—don't be upset. It won't be long now.'

Soon, they came to the candy aisle and the little girl began to shout for candy. When told she couldn't have any, she began to cry.

The mother said, 'There, there, Mary, don't cry—only two more aisles to go and then we'll be checking out.'

When they got to the checkout stand, the little girl immediately began to clamour for gum and burst into a terrible tantrum upon discovering there'd be no gum purchased.

The blonde mother said serenely, 'Mary, we'll be through this check out stand in five minutes and then you can go home and have a nice nap.'

A man followed them out to the parking lot and stopped the woman to compliment her. 'I couldn't help noticing how patient you were with little Mary,' he began.

The mother replied, 'I'm Mary—my little girl's name is Jessie.'

After 20 years of marriage the blonde wife and her husband finally achieved sexual compatibility.

They both had headaches!

Two parents take their son on a vacation and go to a nude beach.

The father goes for a walk on the beach and the son goes and plays in the water.

The son comes running up to his mom and says, 'Mummy, I saw ladies with boobies a lot bigger than yours!'

The blonde mom says, 'The bigger they are, the dumber they are.'

So he goes back to play. Several minutes later he comes running back and says,

'Mummy, I saw men with dingers a lot bigger than Daddy's!'

The mom says, 'The bigger they are, the dumber they are.'

So he goes back to play.

Several minutes later he comes running back and says, 'Mummy, I just saw Daddy talking to the dumbest lady I have ever seen!'

## FEATHERED FRIEND

**A** young blonde husband went off searching for work and eventually wired home from his new job.

'Made foreman. Feather in my cap.'

A few days later he wired.

'Made Assistant Manager. Another feather.'

A few days later he wired.

'Made Manager. Another feather.'

After weeks of silence he wired.

'Fired. Send money for bus fare.'

His wife unfeelingly wired back.

'Use feathers and fly home.'

**T**he doctor had to tell the husband that his blonde wife would have to be admitted to a psychiatric hospital.

'I'm afraid her mind's completely gone,' he said.

'I'm not surprised,' said the husband. 'She's been giving me a piece of it every day for the past 15 years.'

## A LETTER FROM A BLONDE SON

**D**ear Dad,

$chool i$ really great. I am making lot$ of friend$ and $tudying very hard.

With all my $tuff, I $imply can't think of anything I need, $o if you would like, you can ju$t $end me a card, a$ I would love to hear from you.

Love,
Your $on.

## AND THE REPLY

**D**ear Son,
I kNOw that astroNOmy, ecoNOmics and oceaNOgraphy are eNOugh to keep even an hoNOur student busy. Do NOt forget that the pursuit of kNOwledge is a NOble task and you can never study eNOugh.

Love,
Dad

**A** young couple, just married, were in their honeymoon suite on their wedding night.

As they undressed for bed the husband, who was a big burly man, tossed his pants to his pretty blonde bride and said, 'Here, put these on.'

She put them on and the waist was twice the size of her body. 'I can't wear your pants,' she said.

'That's right!' said the husband, 'And don't you forget it. I'm the one who wears the pants in this family!'

With that, she flipped him her panties and said, 'Try these on.'

He tried them on and found he could only get them on as far as his kneecaps.

'Hell, I can't get into your panties!' he said.

She said, 'That's right and that's the way it's going to be until your attitude changes!'

**A**fter a hard day at the office a blonde man gets home from work.

When he comes through the door his wife greets him and says, 'Hi, Honey. Notice anything different about me today?'

'Oh, I don't know. You got your hair done.'

'Nope, try again.'

'Oh, you bought a new dress.'

'Nope, keep trying.'

'You got your nails done.'

'No, try again.'

'I give up, I'm too tired to play 20 questions.'

'I'm wearing a gas mask!'

A couple whose passion had waned saw a marriage counsellor and went through a number of appointments that brought little success.

Suddenly at one session the counsellor leaned over, grabbed the pretty blonde wife and kissed her passionately.

'There,' he said to the husband, 'That's what she needs every Monday, Wednesday, Saturday and Sunday.'

'Well,' replied the husband, 'I can bring her in on Mondays and Wednesdays but Saturdays and Sundays are my fishing days.'

Said one blonde wife to another: 'I think the only reason my husband likes to go fishing so much is that it's the only time he hears someone tell him, "Wow, that's a big one!"'

A blonde walks by a travel agency and notices a sign in the window, 'Cruise Special—$99!'

She goes inside, lays her money on the counter and says, 'I'd like the $99 Cruise Special, please.'

The agent grabs her, drags her into the back room, ties her to a large inner tube, then drags her out the back door and downhill to the river, where he pushes her in and sends her floating.

A second blonde comes by a few minutes later, sees the sign, goes inside, lays her money on the counter and asks for the $99 special.

She too is tied to an inner tube and sent floating down the river.

Drifting into stronger current, she eventually catches up with the first blonde.

They float side by side for a while before the first blonde asks, 'Do they serve refreshments on this cruise?'

The second blonde replies, 'They didn't last year.'

# DECISION MAKING

**G**eorge Bush and Colin Powell were sitting in a bar. A blonde walked in and asked the barman, 'Isn't that President Bush and Mr Powell?'

The barman said, 'Yep, that's them.'

So the girl walked over and said, 'Hello. What are you gentlemen doing?'

Bush said, 'We're planning World War III.'

The blonde asked, 'Really? What's going to happen?'

Bush said, 'Well, we're going to kill 10 million Afghans and one bicycle repairman.'

The girl exclaimed, 'Why are you going to kill a bicycle repairman?!'

Bush turned to Powell and said, 'See, I told you no one would worry about the 10 million Afghans!'


**D**espite acts of great heroism, three British soldiers returned from the Falkland Islands without being decorated.

The captain called them into his office to explain.

'I'm afraid there's been a bit of a cock-up in the medals department, chaps,' he said. 'So, instead, the regiment has decided to give you ten pounds sterling for each inch of measurement between any two parts of your bodies.'

The men look at each other and are not sure how to react. The captain continues 'My efficient nurse here,' pointing to a pretty young thing in fetching uniform, 'Will do the measurements.'

This cheers them up a bit and so they agree.

'All right,' says the captain, pointing at the first man, 'Private, which measurement for you?'

'Tip of me toes to the top of me head, sah!'

The blonde nurse pulls out her tape measure and measures him for height.

'It's six foot—72 inches, Captain,' she says.

'That's 720 pounds,' says the Captain. 'Well done, private.'

Turning to the second solider, he says, 'What about you, Corporal?'

'Tip of one hand to the tip of the other, me arms outstretched, sah!'

The blonde nurse takes the tape measure and measures him for span.

She reports, 'Six feet, two inches.'

'That's 740 pounds,' says the captain. 'Very good, corporal.'

Turning to the final man, he says 'Sergeant, how about you?'

'Tip of me dick to me balls, sah!'

'Hmm, why am I not surprised, Sergeant. Prepared to lose a lot of money just to show off your todger to my pretty young nurse here. Very well. Drop your trousers, then.'

The nurse leans forward and puts the tape measure at one end of the man's penis, then looks up and says, 'Captain, there's, ah, nothing at the other end.'

'What!' says the captain. 'Where are your balls, sergeant?'

'Goose Green, Falklands, sah!'

# BLONDES AND THE LAW

Three blondes were all vying for the last available position on the local police force.

The detective conducting the interview looked at the three of them and said, 'So you all want to be a cop, eh?'

The blondes all nodded.

The detective got up, opened a file drawer and pulled out a file folder.

Sitting back down, he opened it up and withdrew a photograph and said, 'To be a detective, you have to be able to DETECT. You must be able to notice things such as distinguishing features and oddities such as scars, etc.'

He stuck the photo in the face of the first blonde and withdrew it after two seconds. 'Now', he said, 'Did you notice any distinguishing features about this man?'

The blonde immediately said, 'Yes, I did. He only has one eye!'

The detective shook his head and said, 'Of course he only has one eye in this picture! It's a PROFILE of his face! You're dismissed!'

The first blonde hung her head and walked out of the office.

The detective then turned to the second blonde, stuck the photo in her face for two seconds, pulled it back and said, 'What about you? Notice anything unusual or outstanding about this man?'

The blonde immediately shot back, 'Yep! He only has one ear!'

The detective put his head in his hand and exclaimed, 'Didn't you hear what I just said to the other lady? This is a PROFILE of the man's face! Of course you can only see one ear!! You're excused, too! You'd never make a good detective!'

The second blonde sheepishly walked out of the office.

The detective turned his attention to the last blonde and said, 'This is probably a waste of time, but . . .'

He flashed the photo in her face for a couple of seconds and withdrew it, saying, 'Alright. Did YOU notice anything distinguishing or unusual about this man?'

The blonde said, 'Yes, I did. This man wears contact lenses.'

The detective frowned, took another look at the picture and began looking at some of the papers in the folder.

He looked up at the blonde with a puzzled expression and said, 'You're absolutely right! His bio says he wears contacts! How in the world could you tell that by looking at this picture?'

The blonde rolled her eyes and said, 'DUH! He has only one eye and one ear, he certainly CAN'T WEAR GLASSES!'

A blonde was taking her new sports car for a drive when she accidentally cut off a truck driver.

He motioned for her to pull over.

When she did, he got out of his truck and pulled a piece of chalk from his pocket.

He drew a circle on the side of the road and gruffly commanded, 'Stand in that circle and DON'T MOVE!'

He then went to her car and cut up her leather seats.

When he turned around she had a slight grin on her face, so he said, 'Oh you think that's funny? Watch this!'

He got a baseball bat out of his truck and broke every window in her car.

When he turned and looked at her she was still smiling. He was furious and so took a knife out and slashed all her tyres.

The blonde was now doubled over with laughter, which just made the truck driver madder.

In an extreme case of road rage he goes back to his truck and pulls out a can of petrol pours it over her car and sets it on fire.

He turned around and she is still laughing so hard she is about to fall down. 'What's so funny?' the truck driver asked the blonde.

She replied, 'Every time you weren't looking, I stepped outside the circle.'

A policeman pulled a blonde over after she'd been driving the wrong way up a one-way street.

Cop: 'Do you know where you were going?'

Blonde: 'No, but wherever it is, it must be bad 'cause all the people were leaving.'

**A** cop was driving down a country road when he saw a car in a ditch.

He got out of his car to see if anyone was in the car.

A blonde popped her head out the window and said, 'Thank god officer! I was in an accident!'

The officer replied with, 'Well I can see that! Are you okay?'

The blonde nodded.

Then the officer looked around and said, 'What happened?'

The blonde looked at him and said, 'It was so strange. I was driving down the road and from nowhere a tree jumped in front of me, so I swerved to the other side and there was another tree, so I swerved again, but another one was there, so one last time I swerved to the other side but the damn tree got me and caused me to go in this ditch!'

The officer started to laugh hard.

'What's so funny?' the blonde asked.

The officer took a second to catch his breath then said, 'Miss, there's no trees on this road for miles ahead. That was your car air freshener swinging back and forth!'


**O** ne day while on patrol, a police officer pulled over a red sports car for speeding.

He went up to the car and asked the driver, who was a beautiful, buxom blonde, to roll down her window.

'I've pulled you over for speeding. Could I see your driver's licence?'

'What's a licence?' replied the blonde.

The officer thought she was playing dumb to get out of the fine and said, 'It's usually in your wallet.'

After fumbling in her bag for a few minutes, the driver managed to find it.

'Now may I see your registration?' asked the policeman.

'Registration? What's that?' asked the blonde.

The officer began to realise that maybe she wasn't

pretending to be dumb, but that she actually was.

'It's usually on your windscreen,' said the cop impatiently.

The officer took her registration and licence details back to his car to contact headquarters to run a few checks.

After a few moments, the dispatcher came back, 'Um . . . is this woman driving a red sports car?'

'Yes,' replied the officer.

'Is she a drop dead gorgeous blonde?' asked the dispatcher.

'Uh . . . yes,' replied the cop.

'Here's what you do,' said the dispatcher. 'Give her licence back and drop your pants.'

'What!? I can't do that. It's inappropriate!' exclaimed the cop.

'Trust me. Just do it,' said the dispatcher.

So the cop goes back to the car, gives the blonde back her stuff and drops his pants.

The blonde looks down and sighs, 'Oh no . . . not another breathalyser.'


The blonde policeman, a disagreeable sort, stops a local farmer on a minor infraction and proceeds to berate the poor man this way and that, dressing him down most unfairly.

After the lecture, which the farmer takes well, the constable starts writing the poor man up.

While he's writing, he keeps swatting at flies circling his head.

'The circle flies bothering you, are they?' says the farmer.

'Why do you call 'em circle flies, old man?'

'We call 'em that on the farm 'cause we find 'em flying around and around the horses' behinds,' says the farmer.

'Are you calling me a horse's arse?' snarls the cop.

'Oh saints, no,' protests the farmer. 'I wouldn't think of such a thing.'

And the blonde cop goes back to writing.

'. . . kinda hard to fool the flies, though,' adds the farmer quietly.

**A** highway patrolman pulled alongside a speeding car on the freeway.

Glancing at the car, he was astounded to see that the lady behind the wheel was knitting!

The trooper cranked down his window and yelled, 'Pull over!'

'No,' the lady yelled back, 'It's a scarf!'

**A** blonde and a lawyer were sitting next to each other on a plane from London to Sydney.

Eventually the blonde went off to sleep.

But the lawyer got bored and woke the blonde, suggesting they play a game.

The blonde refused and went back to sleep.

The lawyer woke her again and asked again to play a game. Again, the blonde refused and went back to sleep.

The lawyer woke her again and pleaded with her. 'Come on, it'll be a of fun!' he said.

'Oh, okay,' said the blonde, 'I'll play.'

The lawyer said, 'I'll ask you a question and if you can't get it right you pay me $5, you then ask me a question and if I can't answer right, I'll give you $5.'

The blonde says she isn't interested. 'Only $5,' she says.

The lawyer says, 'All right, how about I give you $500 for every question I can't get right, but you only pay me $5.'

The blonde says, 'Okay, for $500, I'll play.'

So the lawyer asks her, 'What is the distance from the earth to the moon?'

The blonde says 'I don't know,' and gives the lawyer $5.

The blonde then says to the lawyer, 'My turn. What has three legs when it goes up a hill, but four legs when it goes down?'

The lawyer frowns, thinks for a while, shakes his head, takes out his laptop and surfs the net to find the answer but, after two hours, can't find it. So he e-mails all his friends but none knew the answer.

Finally, he concludes he doesn't know and writes out a cheque for the blonde for $500.

The blonde takes the cheque and goes back to sleep.

The lawyer wakes the blonde and asks, 'Well, what's the answer?'

The blonde reaches into her purse, takes out $5 and gives it to the lawyer . . .

# BLONDES AROUND THE WORLD

Two blondes were travelling through the Dorset countryside when they saw a sign saying, 'CLEAN REST ROOM AHEAD.' So they did.

On a beautiful desert island in the middle of nowhere, two men and one woman from each of the countries in the European Union are stranded.

Three months pass by and several scenarios are being played out.

One Italian man has killed the other for the Italian woman.

The French men and the French woman are enjoying the threesome but they complain about the multitude of foreigners on their island.

The English men are waiting for someone to introduce them to the English woman.

The German men have a strict weekly alternating sex schedule; the gorgeous blonde German woman gets weekends off.

The Belgian men have realised that the Belgian woman is, in fact, a seven-year-old boy and are mighty ashamed of the whole thing.

The Dutch men are fully prepared, in general, to share the woman. However, they are still debating how to ensure that both will have an exactly equal share, how to reduce supervision cost and how to guarantee the woman equal rights.

The Luxembourg men are still recovering from the shock of seeing half the population of Luxembourg stranded on the island. But they will soon start collecting sea-shells on the beach.

The Finnish men took one look at the endless ocean, one look at the Finnish woman and started swimming.

They were soon overtaken by the Portuguese men.

The Danish trio is trying to find folks to join them in an orgy. They gladly accepted the participation of the Finnish woman and are still vainly persuading the Portuguese woman.

The Spanish men heroically began protecting the virginity of the Spanish woman and are constantly and suspiciously spying on one another. Meanwhile, she dances flamenco.

The Austrian men initiated a yodelling contest for the woman; the loser immediately started learning flamenco, as well as Portuguese, Finnish and Danish.

The Greek men are sleeping with each other and the Greek woman is cleaning and cooking for them.

The Swedish woman strips naked, showing that she truly is a blonde and keeps on bitching about female exploitation while the men are sunbathing and waiting for her to tell them what to do.

The Irish began by setting up a distillery for which they received substantial EU-subsidies. They don't recall if sex is in the picture, because it gets sort of foggy after the first few rounds of coconut whiskey. But they're happy that, at least, the English aren't getting any.

The blonde bloke from the bush had just arrived in the big city and was amazed at the enormity of everything.

Having drunk many stubbies on the journey, he sorely needed to relieve himself.

The first door he entered happened to be a large health club and he asked the clerk if he might use the men's room.

The clerk said certainly and told the wide-eyed traveller that the men's room was the third door down the corridor on the left.

Trying to appear sober, he weaved his way down the hallway remembering some of the directions.

When he reached the third door, he turned right instead of left, opened the door and immediately fell into the deep end of a swimming pool.

The clerk, realising the blonde's mistake, ran down the hall and burst through the door, prepared to save him, only to hear him shout, 'Don't flush, I'm in here!'

An American tourist was boasting to a blonde Norwegian he was trying to impress how advanced the Americans are.

'Gee, we've even put a man on the moon.'

'That's nothing,' replied the blonde, 'We're going to put a man on the Sun.'

'Don't be stupid,' said the American,' 'He'll fry before he even gets there.'

'Oh no, he won't. We're sending him at night,' replied the blonde.

Two blonde Australians are flying home from London. Shortly after taking off there is a big explosion and the pilot announces that one of the engines has gone and the flight will take 20 minutes longer.

Not long afterwards the pilot announces that a second engine has failed and the flight time will no longer be accurate.

A few hours later the pilot speaks to the passenger again to say that they are now flying on one engine and gives an even later arrival time.

When the plane finally lands one blonde turns to the other and remarks, 'Just as well the fourth engine kept going or we'd have been up there for a week.'

Two blonde adventurers were on holiday in the United States and went to see Niagara Falls.

Over drinks one night, one bet the other $500 he couldn't carry him across the falls on a tightrope.

After a very scary trip his friend managed to deposit him safely at the far end and the $500 was duly handed over.

'Pity,' said the loser, 'When you wobbled half way across I was sure I had won.'

A man had been admitted to the local hospital with dysentery after a safari trip to Africa.

He had spent three miserable days on a liquid diet trying to recuperate and smile as best he could while visitors stopped in to wish him well, all the while hoping he didn't have an attack of diarrhoea.

The nurse knocked on his door, peeked in and informed him that he had more visitors on the way up.

As he lay in bed and readied himself for the visit, a sudden onslaught of diarrhoea caught him by surprise, making a mess of his hospital gown and bed sheets.

Not wanting to be embarrassed when his visitors showed up, he quickly took off his hospital gown and ripped the sheets off the bed, tossed them out the window and ran into his bathroom to clean up and put on another hospital gown.

Unbeknown to him, the local blonde drunk had just left the pub and was staggering along the street below his window, when the hospital gown and sheets fell on top of him.

Thinking he had been attacked, the drunk spun around,

covered by the sheets, swinging his arms and punching out at his 'attacker'.

When he finally managed to knock the sheets off, he fell backwards on his behind and sat staring at the pile of sheets in awe.

Just then, a city policeman happened along.

Trying to comprehend the sight before him, he asked him, 'And, just what in the hell happened here?'

The blonde man replied, 'I don't know, sir; but, I think I just beat the shit out of a ghost!'

Fifteen minutes into a flight from Madrid to London, the plane encounters a serious problem with instrumentation.

In a fit of panic, the blonde pilot turns to his co-pilot and says, 'We will have to turn back. None of the navigational equipment is working!'

His blonde assistant replies, 'No problem. I can tell where we are by sticking my hand out the window!'

'Okay,' says the pilot, 'Where are we then?'

The blonde winds down the window and sticks his hand out and replies, 'I reckon we're over the Bay of Biscay. The humidity seems to be gone out of the air. This is caused by the seawater. Just head north.'

'Brilliant!' replies the pilot and proceeds northbound.

An hour later he asks, 'Where are we now?'

The blonde winds down the window and sticks his hand out and replies, 'We're over the English Channel now. The air is much cooler here. Just head in a north westerly direction.'

Thirty minutes later the pilot asks, 'Where are we now?'

He winds down the window and sticks his hand out and replies, 'We're over the East London flats. Quick. Bank left here and you should be on course for Runway One.'

The pilot responds and five minutes later the plane lands safely on Runway One.

He turns to his assistant and says, 'That was brilliant, but tell me, how did you know we were over the East London flats?'

'Well,' said the blonde, 'When I pulled my hand back in, my watch was gone!'

As soon as she had finished school, a bright young blonde girl named Lena made her way to New York where before long, she became a successful performer in show business.

Eventually she returned to her hometown for a visit and on a Saturday night went to confession in the church which she had always attended as a child.

In the confessional Father Sullivan recognised her and began asking her about her work. She explained that she was an acrobatic dancer and he wanted to know what that meant.

She said she would be happy to show him the kind of thing she did on stage.

She stepped out of the confessional and within sight of Father Sullivan, she went into a series of cartwheels, leaping splits, handsprings and back flips.

Kneeling near the confessional, waiting their turn, were two middle-aged ladies.

They witnessed Lena's acrobatics with wide eyes and one said to the other, 'Will you just look at the penance Father Sullivan is giving out tonight and me without me bloomers on!'

A young blonde was on vacation in the north of Queensland. She was desperate for a pair of genuine crocodile shoes but was reluctant to pay the high prices the local vendors were asking.

After becoming very frustrated with the 'no haggle' attitude of one of the shopkeepers, the blonde shouted, 'Maybe I'll just go out and catch my own crocodile so I can get a pair of shoes at a reasonable price!'

The shopkeeper said, 'By all means, be my guest. Maybe you'll be lucky and catch yourself a big one!'

Determined, the blonde turned and headed for the mangroves, set on catching herself a crocodile.

Later in the day, the shopkeeper was driving home, when he spotted the young woman standing waist deep in the water, shotgun in hand.

Just then, he saw a huge four metre crocodile swimming quickly towards her.

She took aim, killed the creature and with a great deal of effort hauled it on to the banks of the mangrove.

Lying nearby were several more of the dead creatures.

The shopkeeper watched in amazement.

Just then the blonde flipped the crocodile on its back and frustrated shouted out, 'Damn it, this one isn't wearing any shoes either!'

**A** blonde woman and her husband go to Mexico City for vacation and go to a famous local restaurant.

They ask the waiter's opinion about what to order and he tells them they have a special each Sunday that's wonderful, so the couple orders that.

With great fanfare, the waiter brings out a large silver serving platter with two huge steaming rounds of meat, juices dripping; it smells delicious and tastes even better.

The couple are delighted with their meal and ask the waiter just what the fabulous meat dish was.

'Senor,' he explains, 'Each Saturday night, we have the bullfights and that was the bull's balls you ate.'

The couple are a bit taken aback by what they had just eaten, but it was delicious, so they get over it.

Six months later, the couple returns to Mexico City and decides to go to the same restaurant.

Feeling adventuresome, they order the same dish.

Once again, with great fanfare, the waiter brings out the huge silver serving dish and places it on the table.

But this time there are two tiny pieces of meat, barely enough for one.

The man says, 'Excuse me, but the last time we were here and ordered this dish, it was huge, more than enough for two. Why is this one so small?'

The waiter smiles and replies, 'Well you see, senor, sometimes the bull wins!'

# BLONDE HEAVEN

A newly deceased man, Ray, stands at the pearly gates. St Peter tells him that he cannot go to heaven right away because he cheated on his income taxes.

The only way he might get into heaven would be to sleep with an ugly woman for the next five years and enjoy it.

Ray decides that this is a small price to pay for an eternity in heaven.

So off he goes with this woman, pretending to be happy.

As he walks along, he sees his friend Marcus up ahead with an even uglier woman. When he asks what's going on, Marcus replies, 'I cheated on my income taxes and scammed the government out of a lot of money.'

They both nod their heads in understanding and figure that they might as well hang out together to help pass the time.

Now Marcus, Ray and their two ugly women are walking along, when they see someone who looks like their old friend Russell up ahead.

This man is with an absolutely gorgeous blonde. She is centrefold material, her beautiful blonde hair framing a perfect face and cascading down over magnificent breasts.

Stunned, Marcus and Ray approach the man and discover it is, indeed, their friend Russell. They ask him how it is he's with this unbelievable goddess, while they're stuck with these god-awful women.

Russell replies, 'I have no idea, but I'm definitely not complaining. This has been absolutely the best time of my life and I have five years of the best sex any man could hope to look forward to. There is only one thing that I can't seem to understand. Every time we finish having sex, she rolls over and murmurs to herself, "Damn income taxes!".'

The priest was saying his goodbyes to the parishioners after his Sunday morning service as he always does, when a blonde woman came up to him in tears.

'What's bothering you so, dear?' inquired Father O'Grady.

'Oh, father, I've got terrible news,' she replied.

'Well what is it?'

'My husband, passed away last night, Father.'

'Oh,' said the father, 'that's terrible. Tell me, did he have any last requests?'

'Well, yes he did father,' replied the woman.

'What did he ask?'

She replied, 'He said, "Please, honey, put down the gun".'

There once was a proud blonde Irishman named Pat, who went to heaven and met St Peter at the Pearly Gates.

St Peter asked, 'Who are you?' and Pat replied,

'My name is Pat, I'm blonde, I'm an Irishman, born on St Patrick's Day, died on St Patrick's Day, while marching in the St Patrick's Day parade.'

St Peter said to Pat, 'Yes, this is true and a worthy claim! Here's a little green cloud for you to drive around heaven in and here is a harp that, when you push this button here, will play "When Irish Eyes Are Smiling". Enjoy it, Pat. Have a good time in heaven.'

Pat jumps on his little green cloud, punches the button and heads out with a smile on his face and a song in his heart.

He's having a wonderful time in heaven, driving his little green cloud around.

But on the third day, he's driving down Expressway H-1 with the harp playing full blast when, all of a sudden, a Jewish man in a pink and white two-tone cloud with tail fins roars past him.

And in the back of this cloud is an organ which is playing all sorts of celestial music.

Pat makes a U-turn right in the middle of the Heaven Expressway and charges back to the Pearly Gates.

He says, 'St Peter, my name is Pat, I'm a proud Irishman, I'm blonde, I was born on St Patrick's Day, died on St Patrick's Day, marching in the St Patrick's Day parade. I come up here to heaven and I get this tiny, insignificant little green cloud and this little harp that plays only one song, "When Irish Eyes Are Smiling". But, there's a Jew over there. He's got a big, beautiful pink and white two-tone cloud and a huge organ that plays all kinds of celestial music and I, Pat the Irishman, want to know why!'

St Peter stands up from his desk.

He leans over and motions Pat to come closer.

Then he says, 'Pat, shush! He's the Boss' Son!'

# BLONDES IN BUSINESS

A blonde was filling out an application form for a job. She promptly filled the columns entitled NAME, AGE, ADDRESS, etc.

Then she came to the column, SALARY EXPECTED.

She answered, 'Yes.'

A blonde who lived in Staten Island, New York and worked in Manhattan, used to take the ferryboat home every night.

One evening, she got down to the ferry and found there was a wait for the next boat, so she decided to have a drink at a nearby bar.

Soon, one champagne rolled into another.

When she got back to the jetty, she spotted a ferry three metres from the dock.

Afraid of missing this one and being late home, she took a running leap and landed right on the deck of the boat.

Turning to a deck-hand, she said proudly, 'How did you like that jump?'

'It was great,' said the sailor. 'But why didn't you wait, m'am? We were just pulling in . . .!'

A blonde burglar has just made it into the house he's intending ransacking and he's looking around for stuff to steal.

All of a sudden, a little voice pipes up, 'Jesus is watching you!'

Startled, the burglar looks around the room. No one there at all, so he goes back to his business.

'Jesus is watching you!'

The burglar jumps again and takes a longer look around the room.

Over in the corner by the window, almost obscured by curtains, is a cage in which sits a budgie, who pipes up again, 'Jesus is watching you!'

'What's your name?' asks the burglar.

'Moses,' the bird replied.

'What kind of an idiot would call a budgie Moses?'

'The same one who would call a Rottweiler Jesus!'

The phone rang at the motor pool and an authoritative voice demanded to know how many vehicles were operational.

The blonde officer at the desk answered, 'Ah, sir, we've got 12 trucks, ten utilities, three staff cars and that Bentley the fat-arsed colonel swanks around in.'

There was a stony silence for a second or two.

'Do you know who you are speaking to?'

'No,' said the blonde.

'It is the so-called fat-arsed colonel you so insubordinately referred to.'

'Well, do you know who you are talking to?'

'No,' roared the colonel.

'Well thank goodness for that,' said the blonde, as she hung up the phone.

Juan comes up to the Mexican border on his bicycle. He's got two large bags over his shoulders.

The blonde guard stops him and says, 'What's in the bags?'

'Sand,' answered Juan.

The guard says, 'We'll just see about that. Get off the bike.' The guard takes the bags and rips them apart; he empties them out and finds nothing in them but sand.

He detains Juan overnight and has the sand analysed, only to discover that there is nothing but pure sand in the bags.

The guard releases Juan, puts the sand into new bags, hefts them onto the man's shoulders and lets him cross the border.

A week later, the same thing happens. The guard asks, 'What have you got?'

'Sand,' says Juan.

The guard does his thorough examination and discovers that the bags contain nothing but sand.

He gives the sand back to Juan and Juan crosses the border on his bicycle.

This sequence of events is repeated every day for three years.

Finally, Juan doesn't show up one day and the guard meets him in a cantina in Mexico.

'Hey, Buddy,' says the blonde guard, 'I know you are smuggling something. It's driving me crazy. It's all I think about ... I can't sleep. Just between you and me, what are you smuggling?'

Juan sips his beer and says, 'Bicycles.'

## A LETTER FROM A BLONDE FARMER TO THE TAX OFFICE EXPLAINING WHY HE HAD NEGLECTED TO PAY HIS TAXES:

**D**ear Sirs,
Your letter arrived this morning and it would have given me pleasure had it not revived in me a melancholy reflection of what has gone before. You say you thought the account could have been settled long ago and you could not understand why it hadn't.

Well, here are the reasons:

1987    I purchased a hay shed on credit.

1988    I bought a combine harvester, a manure spreader, two horses, a double barrel shifter, two cows and ten razor-back pigs, also on credit.

1989    The bloody hay shed burnt to the ground leaving not a damn thing. I got no insurance either as the bloody premium had lapsed. One of the horses went lame and I loaned the other one to my brother who starved the poor bugger to death.

1990    My father died and my brother was put away when he tried to marry one of his sheep named Hilda. A knacker got my daughter pregnant and I had to pay him a grand to stop him becoming one of my relatives.

1991    My son got the mumps which spread to his balls and he had to be castrated to save his life. Later in the year

I went fishing and the bloody boat overturned, drowning two of my sons, neither being the bloody eunuch who was by now wearing his sister's make-up and dresses.

1992    My wife ran away with a pig jobber and left me with newborn twins as a souvenir and I had to get a housekeeper, so I married her to keep down expenses. I had a hell of a job getting her pregnant (to qualify for more children's allowance). I went to see the doctor. He advised me to create some excitement at the crucial moment, so that night I brought my shotgun to bed and when I thought the moment was right I leaned out of bed and shot both barrels through the window. The wife shit the bed, I ruptured myself and the next morning I found I had blown both doors off the barn, shot my best dairy cow and killed the bloody knacker who was in the hay loft with my daughter trying to get more money out of me, which he did because I had to pay for the bastard's funeral expenses.

1993    Someone cut the balls off my prize bull, poisoned the water and set fire to the house. I was bollixed and took to the drink and did not stop until all I had left was a pocket watch and a weak bladder. Winding the watch and running for a piss kept me busy for a time.

1994    I took heart again and bought (on the hire purchase) a bulldozer, tractor and trailer and a new bull. Then the river flooded and washed the bloody lot away, my second wife got VD from a land inspector and my last surviving son died from wiping his arse on a poisoned rabbit. I also had to put down four dogs that were worrying the sheep.

It surprises me very much that you say you will cause trouble if I don't pay up. If you can think of anything I've missed, I should like to know about it. Trying to get money out of me will be like trying to poke butter up a hedgehog's hole with a red hot needle. I'm praying for a cloud of cat's shit to pass your way and I hope it will fall on you and the bastards in your office who sent me this final demand.

Yours for more credit,
The farmer, Murphy

# BLONDES IN PUBLIC PLACES

A blonde taxi passenger tapped the driver on the shoulder to ask him something.

The driver screamed, lost control of the car, nearly hit a bus, went up on the footpath and stopped centimetres from a shop window.

For a second everything went quiet in the cab, then the driver said, 'Look m'am, don't ever do that again. You scared the daylights out of me!'

'I'm so sorry,' said the blonde. 'I didn't realise that a little tap could scare someone so much.'

The driver replied, 'Well, it's not really your fault. Today is my first day as a cab driver. For the previous 25 years, I've been driving hearses . . .'

One day a neighbour was walking past a blonde's house and was surprised to see her crying.

She asked her what had happened, only to find that the blonde's mother had passed away.

The neighbour made her a cup of coffee and eventually calmed her down.

She was just about to leave when the phone rang.

After a short conversation the blonde once again burst into hysterical tears.

Concerned, the neighbour asked what was wrong,

'I just got off of the phone with my sister,' said the blonde. 'Her mother died too!'

**A** blonde was shopping at the supermarket.
As she placed her groceries on the checkout stand, the assistant asked her, 'Paper or plastic?'

'It doesn't matter' she replied, 'I'm bisacksual.'

**I** know a blond so stupid, I asked her to take me to the airport.

We were on the freeway, when she looked up at the sign which said 'Airport Left', so she turned around and went home.

**I** t was a really, really hot day and this blonde decided she would go buy a drink.

She went to the vending machine and when she put her money in, a can of drink came out—so she kept putting money in.

It was such a hot day, a line began forming behind her. Finally, a guy on line said, 'Will you hurry up? We're all hot and thirsty!'

And the blonde said, 'No way. I'm still winning!'

Five blondes appeared in court, each accusing the others of causing the trouble they were having in the apartment building where they lived.

The women were arguing noisily even in the court.

The judge, banging his gavel to quiet them, said, 'We are going to do this in an orderly manner. I can't listen to all of you at once. I'll hear the oldest first.'

The case was dismissed for lack of testimony . . .

'Diabetes,' the lecturer said, 'Is a Greek name; but the Romans noticed that bees like the urine of diabetics, so they added the word mellitus which means sweet as honey. Well, as you know, you may find sugar in the urine of a diabetic . . .'

He asked the nurse to fetch him a sample of urine and when she returned with it he held it high like a trophy.

He dipped a finger boldly into the urine, then licked his finger with the tip of his tongue.

As if tasting wine, he opened and closed his lips rapidly.

Could he perhaps detect a faint taste of sugar?

The sample was passed on to the group of blonde students for an opinion.

They all dipped a finger into the fluid and foolishly licked that finger.

'Now,' said the Registrar grinning, 'You have learned the first principle of diagnosis. I mean the power of observation.'

They were baffled.

'You see,' the registrar said continuing triumphantly, 'I dipped my middle finger into the urine, but licked my index finger—not like all you people did.'

By the time a blonde Marine pulled into a little town, every hotel room was taken.

'You've got to have a room somewhere,' he pleaded. 'Or just a bed, I don't care where.'

'Well, I do have a double room with one occupant—an Air Force guy,' admitted the manager, 'And he might be glad to split the cost. But to tell you the truth, he snores so loudly that people in adjoining rooms have complained in the past. I'm not sure it'd be worth it to you.'

'No problem,' the tired Marine assured him. 'I'll take it.'

The next morning the Marine came down to breakfast bright-eyed and bushy-tailed. 'How'd you sleep?' asked the manager.

'Never better.'

The manager was impressed. 'No problem with the other guy snoring, then?'

'Nope, I shut him up in no time,' said the Marine.

'How'd you manage that?' asked the manager.

'He was already in bed, snoring away, when I came in the room,' the Marine' explained.

'I went over, gave him a kiss on the cheek, said, 'Goodnight, beautiful,' and he sat up all night watching me.'

# BLONDES IN RELATIONSHIPS

**B**londe's diary
Saw John yesterday evening and he was acting really strangely.

I went shopping in the afternoon with the girls and I did turn up a bit late, so thought it might be that.

The bar was really crowded and loud, so I suggested we go somewhere quieter to talk. He was still very subdued and distracted, so I suggested we go somewhere nice to eat. All through dinner he just didn't seem himself; he hardly laughed and didn't seem to be paying any attention to me or to what I was saying. I just knew that something was wrong.

He dropped me back home and I wondered if he was going to come in; he hesitated, but followed.

I asked him again if there was something the matter but he just half shook his head and turned the television on.

After about ten minutes of silence, I said I was going upstairs to bed.

I put my arms around him and told him that I loved him deeply.

He just gave a sigh and a sad sort of smile.

He didn't follow me up, but later he did and I was surprised when we made love.

He still seemed distant and a bit cold and I started to think that he was going to leave me and that he had found someone else. I cried myself to sleep.'

**B**oy's diary
Swans lost to Hawthorn. Still got a root though!

## OTHER PEOPLE'S WIVES

**A** man walks up to a farmer's house, knocks on the door.
When the blonde woman opens the door, the man asks if she knows how to have sex. Not amused, she slams the door.

Again, the man knocks and again, asks the same question.

Still not amused, she screams at the man to get the hell away.

Later, she tells her husband of the incident.

He offers to stay home the following day just in case.

Sure enough, the next day the same man returns.

The husband hides with his gun while the lady answers the door.

When she is asked again if she knows how to have sex, she answers, 'Yes.'

The man replies, 'Great, give some to your husband the next time you see him  and tell him to keep away from my wife.'


**B**arry gets a call from his blonde girlfriend, Barbie.
'I've got a problem,' says Barbie, 'I've bought this jigsaw puzzle, but it's too hard. None of the pieces fit together and I can't find any edges.'

'What's the picture of?' asks Barry.

'It's of a big rooster,' replies Barbie.

'All right,' says Barry, 'I'll come over and have a look.'

So Barry goes over to Barbie's house.

Barbie takes him into the kitchen where the jigsaw is strewn all over the kitchen table.

Barry takes one look at the jigsaw and turns to Barbie and says, 'For Pete's sake—put the cornflakes back in the box.'

A blonde gay man, finally deciding he could no longer hide his sexuality from his parents, went over to their house and found his mother in the kitchen cooking dinner.

He sat down at the kitchen table, let out a big sigh and said, 'Mum, I have something to tell you. I'm gay.'

His mother made no reply or gave any response and the guy was about to repeat it to make sure she'd heard him, when she turned away from the pot she was stirring and said calmly, 'You're gay—doesn't that mean you put other men's penises in your mouth?'

The guy said nervously, 'Uh, yeah, that's right.'

His mother went back to stirring the pot, then suddenly whirled around, whacked him over the head with her spoon and said, 'Don't you EVER complain about my cooking again!'

## MORE THAN HE BARGAINED FOR

'Get this,' said the bloke to his mates, 'Last night while I was down the pub with you guys, a burglar broke into my house.'

'Did he get anything?' his mates asked.

'Yeah, a broken jaw, six teeth knocked out and a pair of broken nuts. My blonde wife thought it was me coming home drunk.'

## WHAT MARRIAGE DOES TO BLONDES

**B**efore :   You take my breath away.
After:   I feel like I'm suffocating.

**B**efore:   Twice a night.
After:   Twice a month.

**B**efore:   She says she loves the way I take control of a situation.
After:   She called me a controlling, manipulative egomaniac.

**B**efore:   Saturday Night Fever
After:   Monday Night Football

**B**efore:   Don't stop.
After:   Don't start.

**B**efore:   Is that all you're having?
After:   Maybe you should have just a salad, honey.

**B**efore:   It's like I'm living in a dream.
After:   It's like he lives in a dorm.

**B**efore:   Turbocharged.
After:   Jumpstart.

**B**efore:   We agree on everything.
After:   Doesn't she have a mind of her own?

**B**efore:    Charming and Noble.
  After:    Chernobyl.

**B**efore:    Idol.
  After:    Dole.

**B**efore:    I love a woman with curves.
  After:    I never said you were fat.

**B**efore:    He's completely lost without me.
  After:    Why won't he ever ask for directions?

**B**efore:    Time stood still.
  After:    This relationship is going nowhere.

**B**efore:    You look so seductive in black.
  After:    Your clothes are so depressing.

**B**efore:    Oysters.
  After:    Fishsticks.

**B**efore:    I can hardly believe we found each other.
  After:    I can't believe I ended up with someone like you.

**B**efore:    Passion.
  After:    Ration.

**B**efore:    Once upon a time.
  After:    The end.

## SEX AND LOVE

**A** blonde couple was told to individually write a sentence using the words 'sex' and 'love'.

The woman wrote, 'When two people love each other very much, like Bob and I do, it is morally acceptable for them to engage in sex.'

And Bob wrote, 'I love sex.'

## DEADLY PRAYERS

**A** man decided that it was time to teach his son how to say prayers.

After the kid had learned them well enough to say on his own, Dad said he could choose someone special and ask for God's blessing for that person.

The first night the little boy said his prayers, he ended with 'And God, please bless my puppy.'

However, the next morning the little dog ran out the door and was killed by a car.

That night the little kid asked God to bless his cat.

And, sure enough, the next morning the cat slipped out and took on the biggest dog in the neighbourhood and lost.

When the kid asked God to bless his goldfish, sure enough, the next morning the fish was found floating upside down on the top.

That night the little kid ended with, 'God, please give an extra special blessing to my father.'

The father couldn't sleep.

He couldn't eat breakfast in the morning.

He was afraid to drive to work.

He couldn't get any work done because he was petrified.

Finally quitting time came and he walked home, expecting to drop dead any minute.

When he arrived home, the house was a mess.

His beautiful blonde wife was lying on the couch still dressed in her robe.

The dishes from breakfast were still on the table and the father was furious.

He yelled at his wife, telling her that he had had the worst day of his life and she hadn't even gotten dressed.

She looked at him and began crying, 'Please don't yell at me, darling. My day was bad, too. Freddy the mailman had a heart attack and dropped dead on the front porch . . .'

## THINGS MEN SHOULD KNOW ABOUT THEIR BLONDE PARTNERS

1. The Female always makes The Rules.
2. The Rules are subject to change at any time without prior notification.
3. No Male can possibly know all The Rules.
4. The Female is never wrong.
5. The Female can change her mind at any given point in time.
6. If the Female has PMS, all The Rules are null and void!

## IRON THIS

Two strangers, a blonde man and a woman, are sitting next to each other on a trans-Atlantic flight.

Suddenly, the plane plummets out of control.

In panic, the woman turns to the man, tears off her blouse and cries,

'Make me feel like a woman one more time!'

Rising to the occasion, the man tears off his shirt and says, 'Here, iron this.'

# WHAT A BLONDE WOMAN REALLY MEANS WHEN SHE ADVERTISES ON AN INTERNET DATING SITE:

| Code word | Means |
| --- | --- |
| 40-ish | 48 |
| Adventurer | Has had more partners than you ever will |
| Affectionate | Possessive |
| Artist | Unreliable |
| Athletic | Flat-chested |
| Average looking | Ugly |
| Beautiful | Pathological liar |
| Commitment-minded | Pick out curtains, now! |
| Communication important | Just try to get a word in edgewise |
| Contagious Smile | Bring your penicillin |
| Educated | College dropout |
| Emotionally Secure | Medicated |
| Employed | Has part-time job stuffing envelopes at home |
| Enjoys art and opera | Snob |
| Financially Secure | One pay check from the street |
| Free spirit | Substance user |
| Friendship first | Trying to live down reputation as slut |
| Gentle | Comatose |
| Good Listener | Borderline Autistic |
| Intuitive | Your opinion doesn't count |
| Light drinker | Lush |
| Looks younger | If viewed from far away in bad light |
| Loves Travel | If you're paying |
| New-Age | All body hair, all the time |
| Non-traditional | Ex-husband lives in the basement |
| Old-fashioned | Lights out, missionary position only |

| | |
|---|---|
| Open-minded | Desperate |
| Poet | Depressive schizophrenic |
| Professional | Bitch |
| Reliable | Frumpy |
| Romantic | Looks better by candle light |
| Spiritual | Involved with a cult |
| Stable | Boring |
| Tall, thin | Anorexic |
| Tan | Wrinkled |
| Wants soul mate | One step away from stalking |
| Writer | Pompous |
| Young at heart | Toothless crone |

## WHAT THE BLONDE MAN REALLY MEANS WHEN HE ADVERTISES ON AN INTERNET DATING SITE:

| Code word | Means |
|---|---|
| 40-ish | 52 and looking for 25-yr-old |
| Artist | Delicate ego badly in need of massage |
| Distinguished-looking | Fat, grey and bald |
| Educated | Will always treat you like an idiot |
| Free Spirit | Sleeps with your sister |
| Good looking | Arrogant bastard |
| Huggable | Overweight, more body hair than Gentle Ben |
| Open-minded | Wants to sleep with your sister but she's not interested |
| Sensitive | Needy |
| Spiritual | Once went to church with his grandmother at Easter |
| Stable | Occasional stalker, but never arrested |
| Thoughtful | Says 'Please' when demanding a beer |
| Young at heart | Paedophile |

Three blokes are waiting to get into heaven.

One bloke asks another why he's there and he says, 'Well I suspected my wife of having an affair so I rushed home and ran up four flights of stairs to our flat as the lift is buggered, burst into the flat and found my beautiful blonde wife naked in bed. But although I searched the flat upside down I couldn't find a man anywhere I looked, all the time I was getting more and more frustrated and angry so finally I picked up the wife's brand new fridge and threw it out the window. That was when I got a heart attack and I died before the ambulance men could get to me because of some disturbance in the street below. What about you?'

'Well,' says the other man, 'I was walking down the street when this fridge came whistling down and hit me on the head and killed me stone dead!'

He turns to the third man, 'How about you pal?'

'Well,' says he 'I was minding my own business, sitting in this fridge when suddenly . . .'

## REASONS

Man says to God, 'God, why did you make this woman blonde and beautiful?'

God says, 'So you would love her.'

'But God,' the man says, 'Why did you make her so dumb?'

God replies, 'So she would love you.'

A bloke walks into a pub and orders six double vodkas.

The barman says, 'Bad day?'

To which the bloke replies 'Yes, I just found out my brother is gay!'

'Oh, you'll get used to it,' replies the barman.

The following day the man re-enters and again orders six double vodkas.

'Not another bad day?' asks the barman.

'Yes,' replies the man, 'I just found out my other brother's gay too.'

'Have an extra one, on the house,' offers the barman.

Two days later the man returned to the pub, looking more depressed than usual, he sits down and orders six double vodkas.

The barman asks, 'For God's sake, does no one in your family like women?'

'Yes,' replies the man, 'My wife does!'

## A BLONDE'S DICTIONARY OF RELATIONSHIPS

**A**ttraction
The act of associating horniness with a particular person.

**L**ove at first sight
What occurs when two extremely horny, but not entirely choosy people meet.

**D**ating
The process of spending enormous amounts of money, time and energy to get better acquainted with a person whom you don't especially like in the present and will learn to like a lot less in the future.

**B**irth control
Avoiding pregnancy through such tactics as swallowing special pills, inserting a diaphragm, using a condom and dating repulsive men.

**E**asy
A term used to describe a woman who has the sexual morals of a man.

**E**ye contact
A method utilised by one person to indicate that they are interested in another. Despite being advised to do so, many men have difficulty looking a woman directly in the eyes, not necessarily due to shyness, but usually due to the fact that a woman's eyes are not located on her breasts.

**F**riend
A person in your acquaintance who has some flaw which makes sleeping with him/her totally unappealing.

**I**ndifference
A woman's feeling towards a man, which is interpreted by the man to be 'playing hard to get'.

**I**nteresting
A word a man uses to describe a woman who lets him do all the talking.

**I**rritating habit
What the endearing little qualities that initially attract two people to each other turn into after a few months together.

**T**he beautiful blonde came home from a Women's Liberation meeting and told her husband, that the meeting had been about free love.
He said, 'Surely you don't believe in free love?'
She replied, 'Have I ever sent you a bill?'

## TIT FOR TAT

**A** boy and his date were parked on a back road some distance from town, doing what boys and girls do on back roads some distance from town, when the girl—a beautiful, well-stacked blonde—stopped the boy.

'I really should have mentioned this earlier, but I'm actually a hooker and I charge $50 for sex,' she said.

The boy reluctantly paid her and they did their thing.

After a cigarette, the boy just sat in the driver's seat looking out the window.

'Why aren't we going anywhere?' asked the hooker.

'Well, I should have mentioned this before, but I'm actually a taxi driver and the fare back to town is $60.'

## WHAT BLONDES REALLY MEAN

| | |
|---|---|
| Did you come? | Because I didn't. |
| I have something to tell you. | Get tested. |
| I'm a Romantic. | I'm poor. |
| Trust me. | I'm cheating on you. |
| I love you. | You're a good lay. |
| I want to make love to you. | Let's just do it. |
| We need to talk. | I'm pregnant. |
| I had a wonderful time last night. | Who the hell are you? |
| I've been thinking a lot. | You're not as attractive as when I was drunk. |
| I've learned a lot from you. | Next! |
| I think we should see other people. | I have been seeing other people. |
| I still think about you. | I miss the sex. |
| Is there something wrong? | Is it supposed to be this soft? |
| You're so mature. | I hope you're eighteen. |

## JUMP START

The young mechanic came to pick up his blonde girlfriend with a pair of jumper leads holding up his pants instead of a belt.

'Don't you start anything . . .' she warned.

# BUSINESS, BUSINESS . . .

A blonde went into the Bank of England to do some business.

The doorman said, 'I'll pass you to one of the clerks, he will see to you.'

The clerk came forward.

'Sir,' he said, 'Is it for redemption or conversion?'

'I don't think I'm in the right place,' said the blonde. 'I want the Bank of England, not the Church of England.'


At the air show the blonde turned to her partner and said, 'I wouldn't like to be up there in one of those things.'

Her partner replied, 'And I wouldn't want to be up there without one.'


The two Americans were standing side by side on top of the Empire State Building.

A blonde who was nearby turned to them and said, 'It's a shame that we can't see a thing on account of the clouds.'

'Well,' replied one American, 'You may not be able to see well, but it has its benefits. If you fall into the cloud you bounce straight back again.'

'I don't believe you,' replied the blonde.

'It's true. Just you watch.'

And with that the American jumped off the side of the building, disappeared amongst the clouds for a few seconds and then sprang back onto the viewing deck.

'I can't believe my eyes. Do it again.'

And so the American did it again.

'I'd like to try that,' said the blonde and jumped over the side and continued on through the cloud to come to a grizzly end on the pavement below.

The hitherto silent American turned to his friend and said, 'You can be a proper bastard at times, Superman.'

**D**id you hear about the blonde who was given a pair of water skis?

He spent the rest of his life looking for a sloping lake.

**H**ave you heard about the blonde innovation for submarines?

Screen doors to keep the fish out.

**T**wo blonde sailors had always been great pals, one was a gunner and the other was a cook.

The cook had a desire to become a gunner and spent a lot of the time on deck looking at the guns and asking questions.

One day he asked his mate if he would just let him fire one shot.

'No, it is too dangerous and the skipper is sure to hear it,' came the reply.

'He won't hear it if I hold a bucket over the muzzle.'

And so he was allowed to load the gun.

He held the bucket over the muzzle and the shot was fired. Away went the bucket with him hanging on for grim death.

The noise aroused the whole crew.

The skipper stormed onto deck and asked, 'Who the hell fired that?'

'It was the cook.'

'And where is he?'

'He's gone to get a bucket of water, but if he comes back as fast as he went he'll be here any minute.'

**O**ne blonde saw another in the street and asked, 'How did the soccer go?'

'It was a great game and the score was nil all.'

'And what was the score at half time?'

'I don't know. I only got there for the second half.'

'**D**on't jump,' said blonde Paddy to the man on the ledge. 'Think of your wife and children.'

'I don't have a wife and children,' said the man.

'Well think of your parents, then.'

'My parents are dead.'

'Then think of St Patrick.'

'Who's St Patrick?'

'Jump, you bastard.'

**A** blonde and her husband were driving home, when they hit a rabbit.

They both got out of the car and stood over the poor creature.

The blonde and her husband just stood there, when suddenly she said, 'Oh I know.'

She went in the car and rummaged through her purse and came out with what looked like a bottle. She poured it on the rabbit and they both got in the car.

Suddenly the rabbit got up, hopped a little bit and waved, hopped a little and waved, hopped to the top of the hill and waved.

Then he disappeared over it.

The husband just stared at his wife and said, 'Honey, what was that you poured on the rabbit?'

His wife replied, 'Hair restorer with a permanent wave.'

# DOCTOR, DOCTOR

'**I** can't find the cause of your illness,' said the doctor, 'But, I think it may be due to drinking.'

'In that case,' replied the blonde, 'I shall come back when you are sober.'

**A**n overweight blonde went to see her doctor for some advice.

The doctor advised that she run 10 kilometres a day for 30 days.

This, he promised, would help her lose 20 kilos.

The blonde followed the doctor's advice and, after 30 days, she was pleased to find that she had indeed lost the whole 20 kilos.

She phoned the doctor and thanked him for the wonderful advice which produced such effective results.

At the end of the conversation, however, she asked one last question, 'How do I get home, since I am now 300 kilometres away?'

**A** blonde lady is not feeling very well and decides to go to a doctor.

While she is waiting in the doctor's reception room, a nun comes out of the doctor's office. She looks very ashen, drawn and haggard.

The blonde goes into the doctor's office and says to the doctor, 'I just saw a nun leaving who looked absolutely terrible. I have never seen a woman look worse.'

The doctor says, 'I just told her that she is pregnant.'

The blonde is astonished. She puts a hand to her mouth. 'Oh my goodness, is she?'

'No, but it sure cured her hiccups!'

A blonde with two very red ears went to her doctor. The doctor asked her what had happened.

'I was ironing a shirt and the phone rang,' she said. 'But instead of picking up the phone, I accidentally picked up the iron and stuck it to my ear.'

'Jesus!' the doctor exclaimed in disbelief. 'So, what happened to your other ear?'

'The person rang back . . .'

A brunette goes into the doctor's office screaming, 'It hurts all over my body!'

'Where?' he asks. 'Point to where it hurts.'

She points to her shoulder and yells, 'OUCH!'

She then points to her hip and yells, 'OUCH!'

Finally she points to her knee, her eye and her chest and screams in pain, 'OUCH! OUCH!! OUCH!! OUCH!! OUCH!'

The doctor asks her, 'Are you in fact a blonde and have dyed your hair brown?'

She answers, 'Yes, how did you know?'

He answers, 'You have a broken finger.'

This old sugar daddy gets his prescription for Viagra and goes home to get ready for when his wife will arrive.

He takes the Viagra and waits.

An hour goes by, the old man is ready to go, but no wife.

He calls her on the mobile. She says, 'The traffic is terrible. I won't be there for about another hour and a half.'

The man, frustrated, calls his doctor for advice.

'What should I do?' he asks.

The doctor replies, 'It would be a shame to waste it. Do you have a housekeeper around?'

'Yes,' the man replies. 'She's this beautiful blonde with the biggest tits you've ever seen.'

'Well, maybe you can occupy yourself with her instead?' says the Doctor.

The man replies with dismay, 'But I don't need the Viagra with the housekeeper . . .'

A beautiful, voluptuous blonde woman goes to see a gynaecologist.

The doctor takes one good look at this woman and his professionalism is a thing of the past. Right away he tells her to undress.

After she has disrobed he begins to stroke her thigh.

As he does he says to the woman, 'Do you know what I'm doing?'

'Yes,' she says, 'You're checking for any abrasions or dermatological abnormalities.'

'Correct,' says the doctor.

He then begins to fondle her breasts. 'Do you know what I'm doing now?' he says.

'Yes,' says the woman, 'you're checking for any lumps or breast cancer.'

'That's right,' replies the doctor.

He then gradually proceeds to having sexual intercourse with her. 'Do you know,' he pants 'What I'm doing now?'

'Yes,' she says. 'You're getting herpes.'

An evaluation of the drugs, medical procedures and priorities used over the past few years shows that more money has been spent on breast implants and Viagra, than on Alzheimer's Disease research.

As a consequence, the research estimates that by the year 2030 there will be 40,000,000 people wandering around with huge tits and mighty erections who can't remember what to do with them.

This fellow had been suffering from excruciating headaches for some time and finally went to a doctor.

After a thorough exam, the physician called the fellow into his office and said, 'Well, I'm not exactly sure what is causing your headaches, but we've found a cure for them. You'll have to be castrated.'

The man, needless to say, was taken aback and told his doctor that he believed he would try to bear the pain.

But as time went on, the headaches only got worse and finally, the poor fellow was driven back to the doctor.

'All right, I guess I'll have the operation,' he said.

When it was all over, the man was understandably depressed and his physician told him, 'I recommend you begin life anew. Start over from this point.'

So the man decided to take the advice and went to a men's shop for a new set of clothes.

The young blonde sales girl says, 'Starting with the suit, it looks like you take about a 38 regular.'

'That's right,' exclaimed the man, 'How'd you know?'

'Well, when you've been in the business as long as I have, you get pretty good at sizing a man up,' replied the sales girl.

'Now, for a shirt, looks like about a 15 long.'

'Right again,' the man said. 'That's fantastic. I can't believe that you can be so accurate!'

'Well, as well as experience, you can add women's intuition.'

'All right,' says the man, 'I'm feeling a lot better, we may as well buy some underwear, too.'

'Hmmm, jocks,' says the girl. 'I'd say a size 36.'

'There's your first mistake,' the man said, 'I've worn size 34 for years.'

'No, you're a size 36 if I've ever seen one,' said the girl. 'You wear a size 34, they're going to press everything tightly together and you're going to get the most terrible headaches . . .'


The doctor looked benignly at the woman who had come to him for an examination.

'Mrs Brown,' he said, 'I have some good news for you.'

The blonde looked up at him and said, 'I'm glad of that doctor, but I'm Miss Brown,'

'Miss Brown,' said the doctor without changing expression, 'I have bad news for you.'

# EDUCATION

TOP 20 BLONDE BOOKS

- The Royal Family's Guide to Good Marriages.
- Safe Places to Travel in the USA.
- The Code of Ethics for Lawyers.
- The Australian Book of Foreplay.
- The Book of Motivated Postal Workers.
- Americans' Guide to Etiquette.
- Bill Clinton: A Portrait of Integrity.
- The Wit and Wisdom of George W. Bush.
- Cooking Enjoyable Dishes with Tofu.
- The Complete Guide to Catholic Sex.
- Consumer Marketing Ethics.
- Popular Lawyers.
- John Howard: The Bourbon Years.
- Career Opportunities for History Majors.
- Everything Men Know about Women.
- Home Built Airplanes, by John Denver.
- My Life's Memories, by Ronald Reagan.
- Things I Love About Bill, by Hillary Clinton.
- Things I Can't Afford, by Bill Gates.

# GOOD HEAVENS

A surgeon, an architect and a blonde were discussing whose profession was the oldest.

'Eve was made from the rib of Adam,' said the surgeon, 'Surely that was a surgical job.'

'Maybe,' said the architect, 'But prior to that order was created from chaos and that must have been an architectural job.'

'That is all true,' said the blonde, 'But somebody had to create the chaos in the first place.'

The blonde died and went to Heaven.

She was greeted by St Peter who told her that in heaven a million years is counted as a minute and a million dollars is counted as a cent.

'I'm needing cash,' said the blonde, 'Can you lend me a cent?'

'Sure,' said St Peter, 'Just wait a minute.'

The blonde was an inveterate drunk.

His doctor was talking to him about the evil effects of demon drink and, in order to scare him into reforming his ways suggested that the more he drank the smaller he would become. In the end he would be so small that he would turn into a mouse.

The drunk went home and said to his wife, 'Darling, if you notice me getting smaller and smaller, will you kill the blasted cat.'

The priest was having a terrible time avoiding a nervous breakdown and had spent many a session on the blonde psychiatrist's couch.

As a last resort, the good doctor ordered him to forget that he was a priest for a weekend, to go to the city, take the dog collar off, enjoy a few drinks and a bet at the casino and to live it up.

He did that and was having a wonderful time when he walked into a strip joint, sat down and ordered a stiff whisky.

'I'll get that for you straight away, Father,' said the hostess.

The priest panicked.

'How do you know that I am a priest?' he stuttered.

'Oh, I'm Sister Mary, I go to the same psychiatrist as you do.'


Two blondes were talking about a friend who was suffering from a dreadful disease.

'I'm terribly afraid that she's going to die.'

'And what makes you say that?'

'Oh she's got so thin. Now I mean, you're thin and I'm thin. But she's as thin as the two of us together.'


Then there was the blonde Evel Knievel.

He tried to jump over 23 motor bikes in a bus.


'What are those two bulges at the front of your trousers?' asked the barmaid.

'Ah,' said the blonde, 'They are hand grenades. Next time that old queer, Gregory tries to feel me up, I'll blow his bloody hands off.'

It was a dark, dark night and the blonde was making his way home after a rollicking evening at the pub.

He heard a faint cry for help off in the distance and full of good cheer he followed the sound and came across a small wizard who had his foot caught under a large stone.

He released the foot for the wizard and, as a token of his gratitude, the wizard granted him three wishes.

'I'll have a bottle of the best Scotch whisky,' said the blonde.

Sure enough there appeared a bottle of top shelf whisky and the blonde gulped it down.

'And what for your second wish?' asked the wizard.

'Make this a never ending bottle of the good stuff for me.'

With a wave of his wand, his wish was granted.

'And for a third wish?' asked the wizard.

'I'll have another bottle like this,' slurred the blonde.

The blonde, when asked if she spoke French, replied that she did as long as it was spoken in English.

# THIS HAPPENED, HONEST!

These are the answers that drivers gave when claiming on their insurance. They are taken from actual claims and it is reliably believed that the majority of the drivers were blonde.

- Coming home I drove into the wrong house and collided with a tree I don't have.

- The other car collided with mine without giving me warning of its intention.

- I thought my window was down, but I found it was up when I put my head through it.

- I collided with a stationary truck coming the other way.

- A pedestrian hit me and went under my car.

- The guy was all over the road. I had to swerve several times before I hit him.

- I pulled away from the side of the road, glanced at my mother in law and headed over the embankment.

- In an attempt to kill a fly, I drove into a telephone pole.

- I had been shopping for a plant all day and was on my way home. As I reached an inter-section a hedge sprang up, obscuring my vision and I did not see the other car.

- I had been driving for 40 years when I fell asleep at the wheel and had an accident.

- I was on the way to the doctor with rear end trouble when my universal joint gave way causing me to have an accident and damage my big end.

- As I approached the inter-section a sign appeared in a place where no stop sign had ever appeared before. I was unable to stop in time to avoid the accident.

- To avoid hitting the bumper of the car in front I struck a pedestrian.

- My car was legally parked as it backed into another vehicle.

- An invisible car came out of nowhere, struck my car and vanished.

- I told the police that I was not injured, but on removing my hat I found that I had a fractured skull.

- I was sure the old fellow would never make it to the other side of the road when I struck him.

- The pedestrian had no idea which direction to run. So I ran over him.

- I saw a slow moving, sad faced old gentleman as he bounced off the roof of my car.

- The indirect cause of the accident was a little guy in a small car with a big mouth.

- I was thrown from my car as it left the road. I was later found in a ditch by some stray cows.

- The telephone pole was approaching. I was attempting to swerve out of the way when I struck the front end.

- The accident was caused by me waving to the man I hit last week.

- I knocked over a man, he admitted it was his fault as he'd been knocked over before.

# INTUITION

The blonde arrived at work looking very bleary eyed and tired.

'What is wrong with you?' asked her friend.

'I was up half the night,' came the reply.

'And why was that?'

'Well, I had to wait for the cat to come home so I could put her out for the night.'


The blonde was trying to get his donkey under a bridge which was slightly low.

But that didn't deter the blonde. He began to chisel away at the bricks.

'It might be better to dig a few centimetres out of the ground,' came the suggestion.

But the blonde would have nothing of it.

'Use your brains. It's not his feet that's the trouble. It's his ears that won't go.'


Did you hear about the blonde who had a slack clothesline? He had the house moved a metre forward.


The blonde asks her friend did she know that we only use one third of our brains.

'Whatever happens to the other third?' came the reply.

The blonde farmer was taking a donkey to market in order to sell it.

As he was trudging along the road he thought to himself that it was silly to walk when he could take the train.

So he went to the station and waited for the train.

He boarded and was trying to drag his donkey along with him, when the guard told him that he could not do that and he should send the donkey down the back for the journey.

Now the blonde did not understand that he meant the guard's van and so tied the donkey to the back of the train for the journey.

The blonde went back and sat in his carriage and at the end of the journey he went to collect his donkey. But there was no sign of him.

He went to the front of the train and spoke to the driver, 'Did you by any chance notice a donkey pass you?'

'Dad,' said the young boy to his very blonde father, 'Can you help me to blow up the balloons for the party?'

'Certainly not,' said his dad, 'You are far too young to play with explosives.'

Then there was the blonde little terrier sitting in the corner gnawing on a bone. When he stood up, he had only three legs.

The blonde was in a bar and wanted to borrow money from his mate who had a small boy with him.

'That's a fine lad you have there. A great head and strong features. Could you loan me ten quid?'

'I could not,' came the reply, 'This is my wife's son by her first husband.'

Then there was the blonde who was given two weeks to live.

He decided to take one in July and the other in December.

Have you heard about the blonde who thought that manual labour was a Spanish tennis player?

# BLONDE . . . AND IRISH!

**A** young blonde Irish girl goes into her priest on Saturday morning for confession.

'Father, forgive me for I have sinned.'

'You've sinned?'

'Yes, I went out with me boyfriend Friday night. He held me hand twice, kissed me three times and made wild passionate love to me two times.'

'Daughter! I want you to go straight home, squeeze seven lemons into a glass and drink it straight down.'

'Will that wash away me sin?'

'No, but it will get the silly smile off your face.'


**T**hree young Irishmen died at the same time. Upon encountering the Pearly Gates, they were met by St Patrick himself.

He addressed the boys, 'Lads, I'm here to welcome you to heaven where you will spend eternity. Just remember one thing, when you go through these gates, don't step on any of the ducks or you'll be punished for eternity.'

Sean went in first and was amazed to see that the entire landscape was encompassed by ducks and try as he might, he could not avoid stepping on one.

He was immediately joined by the plainest girl he had ever laid eyes on and she said, 'Well love, you stepped on a duck and now we're together for all time.'

The exact same thing happened to Michael, only his companion was even uglier than the first girl.

Tim was absolutely terrified.

He gingerly managed to make it most of the way across the court without stepping on a single duck.

Suddenly, his arm was taken by a beautiful blonde young lass.

Tim looked over and beheld the most beautiful, graceful, blue-eyed woman he's ever seen in all his life.

He gasped, 'I don't understand it!'

The young beauty answered, 'Well I'm sure I don't either, I was walking along minding my own business, when all of a sudden I stepped on a duck . . .'

The blonde Bridget Quinn is the parish's oldest surviving eligible spinster.

Her beauty is fading, but she takes great delight in the fact that she has already outlasted two pastors.

She never gives up hope.

She never seems to run out of man-hunting stunts, either.

Her latest effort—at the parish annual singles dance—was a classic.

She jumped up on the bandstand, her right hand clenched into a fist, raised high and then she saucily announced, 'Any one of you handsome, virile devils who can guess what's in me hand can win a week's worth of romantic, candlelight dinners—just the two of us, me an' you!

Nobody spoke up.

Dead silence.

Then, a witty, older senior gentleman shouts out, 'Is it an elephant?'

Miss Quinn squealed for joy, 'Glory be to God, that's close enough—dinner tis' at seven, me boy!'

Three blonde Irishmen, Paddy, Sean and Seamus, were stumbling home from the pub late one night and found themselves on the road which led past the old graveyard.

'Come have a look over here,' said Paddy, 'It's Michael O'Grady's grave, God bless his soul. He lived to the ripe old age of 87.'

'That's nothing,' said Sean, 'Here's one named Patrick O'Toole. It says here that he was 95 when he died.'

Just then, Seamus yelled out, 'Hey, here's a fella that got to be 145 years old!'

'What was his name?' asked Paddy.

Seamus lit a match to see what else was written on the stone marker and exclaimed, 'Miles, from Dublin.'

Paddy, an Irishman, died in a fire and was burnt pretty badly, so the morgue required someone to identify the body.

His two best friends who were blondes, Seamus and Sean, were sent for.

Seamus went in first and the mortician pulled back the sheet.

Seamus took a look at the body, said, 'Yup, he's burnt pretty bad. It could be him. Roll him over.'

So the mortician rolled him over.

Seamus looked down and said, 'Nope, that ain't Paddy'.

The mortician thought that was rather strange and then he brought Sean in to identify the body. Sean took a look at the corpse and said, 'Gee, he's burnt really bad. Will you roll him over?'

The mortician rolled the body on to its front and Sean looked down for a moment before saying, 'No, it isn't Paddy'.

The mortician, puzzled, asked, 'How can you tell?'

Sean replied, 'Well, Paddy had two blonde arseholes.'

'What do you mean? No one has two blonde arseholes,' said the mortician.

'Yup, everyone knew he had two arseholes. Every time we went into town, folks would say, "Here comes Paddy with them two blonde arseholes!"'

The entire family were at Shannon Airport to see Patrick, his pretty blonde wife Colleen and the children off to Australia.

Patrick thought it a good idea to get a photo of the occasion as a keepsake.

They asked a fellow traveller to take the picture with Patrick's old camera.

The family stood still for what seemed like a lifetime.

They were getting a bit fidgety and Colleen says, 'Sure and what's taking so long, Patrick?'

Patrick says, 'Well love, he's got to focus first.'

Colleen replies, 'What, all of us!'

Seamus O'Malley is playing golf when he takes a hard struck golf ball right in the crotch. Writhing in agony, he falls to the ground. As soon as he could manage, he took himself to Doctor O'Connor.

'How bad is it doctor?' asks O'Malley, 'I'm going on my honeymoon next week and my blonde girlfriend is a virgin in every way.'

'I'll have to put your penis in a splint, Seamus, to let it heal and keep it straight. Sure, it'll be fine by next week.'

The doctor takes four tongue compressors and forms a neat little four-sided bandage and wires it all together.

'An impressive work of art,' says the good doctor.

Seamus says nothing of this to his blonde girl-friend, marries and goes off on his honeymoon.

That night in the hotel room she rips off her blouse to reveal a gorgeous set of breasts, a sight Seamus has not seen before.

'You're the first, Seamus. No one has ever touched these breasts.'

Seamus promptly drops his pants and replies,

'Would you look at this . . . it's so new, it's still in the CRATE!'

A blonde Irishman named Paddy was coming through Customs at the airport carrying a large bottle.

'What's that?' asked a suspicious Customs officer.

''Tis Lourdes holy water,' answered Paddy.

The officer took the lid off the bottle and sniffed it.

'This is whisky!' said the officer.

'Begorrah, another miracle!' said the unflappable Paddy.

A blonde was patiently waiting and watching the traffic cop on a busy street crossing.

The cop stopped the flow of traffic and shouted, 'Okay pedestrians!'

Then he'd stop them and allow the traffic to pass. He did this several times and the blonde still stood on the sidewalk.

After the cop had shouted 'Pedestrians!' for the tenth time, the blonde went over to him and said, 'Is it not about time you let the Catholics across?'

# NO ORDINARY TALENT

A blonde was at a party and showing off her tricks. Holding out her hand she said, 'Pick a thumb, any thumb.'

When her fellow party goer complied, she put her hand behind her back for a moment and then, bringing it forward requested, 'Okay, now which hand is it in?'

In 1789 in Paris, three revolutionaries are about to be executed at the guillotine.

The executioner asks the redhead, 'Do you want to be executed on your front or on your back?'

'On my back,' he replied, 'I am not afraid of death.'

The redhead was laid on his back, but there was a malfunction of the blade and it did not descend far enough to behead him.

He was granted a reprieve.

The brunette was next and he too chose to be executed on his back.

Again the blade failed to operate.

He also was reprieved.

'Back or front?' the executioner asked the third fellow, a blonde.

'If it's good enough for the others then it is good enough for me,' he said, 'I choose to go on my back.'

So he was laid on his back to meet his death.

As he lay there under the blade he spoke to the executioner, 'Ah, I think I can see the problem why the blade sticks, just move it a little to the left.'

Have you heard about the blonde sky diver who was killed when his snorkel and flippers failed to open?

Then there's the new blonde invention. The parachute that opens on impact.

The blonde pilot was in trouble at the controls.
'Mayday, Mayday,' radioed the pilot.
'Cleared to land,' answered the control tower.
'Can I have your height and position?'
'I'm five foot four inches and I am sitting right at the front of the plane, silly!'

A blonde and a brunette jumped off the Eiffel Tower. The brunette got killed and the blonde got lost.

Did you hear about the blonde newlyweds who sat up all night waiting for their sexual relations to arrive?

The older blonde woman was healthy and active, but went to the doctors asking to have a vasectomy.
'Why?' asked the doctor.
'I've got ten grandchildren already and I don't want any more . . .'

The blonde horse trainer had two horses that he could never quite tell apart until one day, when he found that the white horse was two hands shorter than the black one.

One of the simplest devices is the Blonde Mine Sweeper. All you do is put your hands over your ears and tap around at the earth in front of you with your toe.

An international team of medical scientists decided that research should be done into the penis and why it was shaped with a knobbed end. Funds were allocated to three teaching hospitals to carry out the work.

The Royal London Hospital reported first. They had spent over $50,000 and conducted tests on over 6000 subjects. They had given questionnaires to a further 4000 men and had come to the conclusion that the penis was shaped thus as its broader extremities gave additional pleasure during sexual intercourse.

The Paris contingent presented their findings. After spending three million francs, they outlined the responses to over 5000 country men in a 70 page booklet. The French had concluded that the female partner had added sexual pleasure because of the shape of the male penis.

The blonde study team at the Royal Danish Hospital conducted their tests on a sample of five in-house scientists and at very little cost to the institution. Their findings were contained in one paragraph which simply said, 'The knob at the end of the male penis is to stop the hand from slipping off.'

Two blondes are clinging onto the edge of an iceberg.
'We're saved! We're saved.' called the first gleefully.
'How do you know that?' asked the second.
'I can see the Titanic coming towards us.'

Did you hear about the blonde marksman? He fired a shot in the air and missed.

A blonde was walking along the river bank, when she saw a desperate fellow trying to commit suicide by drowning in the river.
Unable to bear the thought she jumped into the water and dragged him out.

However, he was not grateful and intent on finishing the job at hand, he rushed back into the water and began the drowning process again.

Again he was pulled out by the blonde.

In frustration he took a rope from the boot of his car and hanged himself from a nearby tree.

The blonde looked at him hanging there and walked on.

At the inquest, the judge asked the blonde why, after having gone to so much trouble to save the poor man from drowning, she had walked off and left him to die by hanging.

'Your honour,' replied the blonde, 'I thought that he was simply hanging himself out to dry.'

# OBSERVANT

Then there was the blonde grand prix driver who made 100 pit stops.

Four of them were for fuel and the other 96 were asking for directions.

Two drunken blondes stumbled into a funeral parlour. They bumped about until one fell over the piano.

'Here's a coffin,' he told his mate.

'Do you recognise who's in there?' asked his mate.

'No,' admitted the first blonde, 'But he sure had a good set of teeth.'

Two blonde drunks were pulled up by the police.

'And what is your address?' the policeman asked of the first blonde.

'I'm Tom Smith and I have no fixed address.'

'And you?' said the cop, turning to the other blonde.

'My name is Peter Jones and I live in the flat above his.'

A blonde walks into a bar.

'Good evening, sir and what can I help you with this evening?'

'I'll have a scotch and a box of matches, please.'

He then puts five cents on the bar and drinks the scotch.

'What's the five cents for?' asks the barman.

'That's for the matches. I didn't really want a drink, but you asked me so nicely that I felt obliged to drink it.'

'Sir, I was only being polite. You have to pay.'

'I'm sorry, but I didn't really want the drink and I refuse to pay.'

He is barred from the pub.

Two weeks later he walks back into the same bar.

The barman sees him and shouts, 'Out! We do not want you in here. I told you never to return again!'

The chap refuses and tells the barman that he must have mixed him up with somebody else as he has been out of the country and has only just returned that day.

The barman takes a closer look at him and says almost to himself, 'I don't understand it. You must have a double.'

'Thanks mate and I'll have a packet of matches as well . . .'

Then there was the blonde yachty who could never win a race because they always put something in the water.
The other yachts.

The two blonde fishermen sprung a leak in one end of their boat.

'Not to worry,' said one to the other, making a hole in the other end of the boat, 'This will let the water out.'

Did you hear about the blonde water polo team?
They drowned the horses.

When asked whether she wanted her pizza cut into four or six, the blonde said, 'Make it four, I don't think I could eat six.'

The first blonde steeplechase had to be abandoned as no one could get a proper grip on the roof.

The blonde astronaut is developing a rocket, but he is having trouble finding a bottle big enough for the stick.

# PC

## POLITICALLY CORRECT TERMS OF ENDEARMENT FOR BLONDES

| | |
|---|---|
| Creatively Re-Dyed | blonde |
| Chronologically Gifted | old |
| Biologically Challenged | dead |
| Caucasian Culturally Disadvantaged | white trash |
| Certified Astrological Consultant | crackpot |
| Certified Crystal Therapist | crackpot |
| Certified Past-Life Regression Hypnotist | crackpot |
| Differently Organised | messy |
| Differently Brained | stupid |
| Facially Challenged | ugly |
| Factually Unencumbered | ignorant |
| Financially Inept | poor |
| Gravitationally Challenged | fat |
| Horizontally Challenged | thin |
| Horizontally Gifted | fat |
| In Recovery | drunk/junkie |
| Intellectually Impaired | stupid |
| Living-Impaired | dead |
| Metabolically Challenged | dead |
| Monetarily Challenged | poor |
| Morally Challenged | a crook |
| Motivationally Challenged | lazy |
| Musically Delayed | tone deaf |
| Nasally Disadvantaged | really big nose |
| Nasally Gifted | large nose |

## ADULTS ONLY BLONDE JOKES

| | |
|---|---|
| Outdoor Urban Dwellers | homeless |
| Persons Living With Entropy | dead |
| Sanitation Engineer | garbage man |
| Sexually Focused Chronologically Gifted Individual | dirty old man |
| Socially Challenged | geek, nerd |
| Spatially Perplexed | drunk |
| Uniquely Coordinated | clumsy |
| Vertically Challenged | short |
| Visually Challenged | blind |

# Q & A

**Q.** How do you make a blonde laugh on a Monday?
**A.** *Tell her a joke on a Friday.*

**Q.** What do you call a blonde man with no arms and no legs who can play the drums?
**A.** *Clever Dick.*

**Q.** How many blondes does it take to hit a nail into a wall?
**A.** *Twenty-two. One to hold the hammer, one to hold the nail and twenty to shove the wall forward.*

**Q.** How is a ladder used by a blonde workman different from other ladders?
**A.** *It has a stop sign on the top.*

**Q.** How do you confuse blondes?
**A.** *Give them a box of M&M's and tell them to put them in alphabetical order.*

**Q.** How do you confuse a blonde workman?
**A.** *Put three spades into a corner and tell him to take his pick.*

**Q.** Why did the blonde golfer have two pairs of pants?
**A.** *In case he got a hole-in-one.*

**Q.** How do you confuse blondes?
**A.** *Give them a box of Jaffas and tell them to eat the red ones last.*

**Q.** Why was the blonde pleased with herself when she finished the jigsaw in six months?

**A.** *Because it said on the cover 'Three to Five Years.'*

**Q.** What does a maths graduate say to a sociology graduate?

**A.** *I'll have the burger and fries, please.*

**Q.** When is it much better to be a woman than a man?

**A.** *When you are in the lavatory and the plane hits turbulence.*

**Q.** What's the difference between Jewish women and Catholic women?

**A.** *Catholic women have fake jewellery and real orgasms.*

**Q.** Why did the blondes climb the glass wall?

**A.** *To see what was on the other side.*

**Q.** What do you call six blondes standing in a circle?

**A.** *A dope ring.*

**Q.** How do blondes like their eggs?

**A.** *Fertilised.*

**Q.** What is the difference between a blonde and the Titanic?

**A.** *We know how many went down on the Titanic.*

**Q.** Why is it unwise to give a blonde more than ten minutes for lunch break?

**A.** *Because any longer and you would have to retrain her.*

**Q.** Why do blondes have lunch boxes with clear lids?
**A.** *So that they will know whether they are coming or going to work.*

**Q.** Why don't Baptists make love standing up?
**A.** *Because it might lead to dancing.*

**Q.** What's grey, has four legs and a trunk?
**A.** *A mouse on vacation.*

**Q.** How are sex and air a lot alike?
**A.** *Neither one's a big deal unless you're not getting any.*

**Q.** How do you make an elephant fly?
**A.** *Start with a 3 foot zipper . . .*

**Q.** How do you know when you pass an elephant?
**A.** *You can't get the toilet seat down.*

**Q.** What's the red stuff between elephant's toes?
**A.** *Slow pygmies.*

**Q.** What is more difficult than getting an elephant into the back seat of your car?
**A.** *Getting a pregnant elephant in the back seat of your car.*

**Q.** What is more difficult than getting a pregnant elephant in the back of your car?
**A.** *Getting an elephant pregnant in the back seat of your car.*

**Q.** Dad, what's a transvestite?

**A.** *I don't know, but ask your Mother, he'll know!*

**Q.** What happens if you play a country and western song backwards?

**A.** *The singer gets his wife, house and his job back!*

**Q.** What's the mating call of a blonde.

**A.** *'I think I'm drunk.'*

**Q.** What is the mating call of a brunette?

**A.** *'Has that dumb blonde gone yet?'*

**Q.** If a bra is an upper topper flopper stopper and a jock strap is a lower decker pecker checker and golden toilet paper is a super duper pooper scooper, then what is a Japanese boxer with a father who has diarrhoea??

**A.** *A slap happy Jappy with a crap happy pappy.*

**Q.** When does a blonde enjoy a man's company?

**A.** *When she owns it.*

**Q.** What did the blonde Leper say to the Prostitute?

**A.** *You can keep the tip.*

**Q.** Why do blondes drive BMWs?

**A.** *Because they can't spell Porsche.*

**Q.** Why did the blonde leper fail her driving test?

**A.** *She left her foot on the clutch.*

**Q.** Did you hear about the short-sighted circumciser?

**A.** *He got the sac.*

**Q.** What are a blonde's four favourite animals?
**A.** *A mink in the closet, a Jaguar in the garage, a tiger in the bedroom and a jackass who'll pay for it all.*

**Q.** How did Pinocchio find out he was made of wood?
**A.** *His hand caught fire.*

**Q.** What did the blonde call his pet zebra?
**A.** *Spot.*

**Q.** How many blondes does it take to make a chocolate chip biscuit?
**A.** *Thirteen. One to mix the dough and 12 to peel the smarties.*

**Q.** What did God say after creating Man?
**A.** *I must be able to do better than that.*

**Q.** What did God say after creating Eve?
**A.** *Practice makes perfect.*

**Q.** What did God say after creating the first blonde?
**A.** *I think I might come to regret this.*

**Q.** How are men and parking spots alike?
**A** *All the good ones are always taken. Free ones are mostly handicapped or extremely small.*

**Q.** What is the one thing that all men at singles bars have in common?
**A.** *They're married.*

**Q.** Did you hear about the cannibal who had chronic indigestion?
**A.** *He ate someone who disagreed with him.*

**Q.** What do you get if you cross a dog with a Concorde?
**A.** *A jet setter.*

**Q.** How do you give a
blonde bloke a brain
transplant?
**A.** *Blow through his
ear.*

**Q.** Why do blondes
wear green lipstick?
**A.** *Because red means
'Stop'.*

**Q.** Why are bull sperm and politicians the same?
**A.** *In each case, only one in a thousand works!*

**Q.** What do a Christmas tree and a Catholic priest have in
common?
**A.** *Their balls are just for decoration.*

**Q.** What does DNA stand for?
**A.** *National Dyslexics Association.*

**Q.** How do blonde brain cells die?
**A.** *Alone.*

**Q.** How many blondes does it take to change a light bulb?
**A.** *Only one. He holds the light bulb and the world
revolves around him.*

**Q.** Did you hear the one about the Dyslexic Pimp?
**A.** *He bought a warehouse!*

**Q.** Did you hear about the Dyslexic Devil Worshipper?
**A.** *He sold his soul to Santa!*

**Q.** What is a definition of a pessimist?
**A.** *Someone who takes a daily dish of prunes with his All Bran.*

**Q.** Why was the washing machine laughing?
**A.** *Because it was taking the piss out of the knickers.*

**Q.** Why do nursing homes give Viagra to old men?
**A.** *To stop them rolling off the bed.*

**Q.** How can you tell if a blonde has been using your computer?
**A.** *There is liquid paper all over the screen.*

**Q.** Why do blondes have TGIF written on their shoes?
**A.** *So they know that their Toes Go In First.*

**Q.** Why do blondes like to swim under water?
**A.** *Because deep down they are intelligent.*

**Q.** What is the first thing that a blonde does in the morning?
**A.** *She gets dressed and goes home.*

**Q.** What do you call a brunette who is standing between two blondes?
**A.** *An interpreter.*

**Q.** What does a blonde call a bottle of black hair dye?
**A.** *Artificial intelligence.*

**Q.** How do you know that a blonde has been using your electric shaver?

**A.** *There is shaving cream all over the bathroom.*

**Q.** What do blondes and cow pats have in common?

**A.** *The older they get the easier they are to pick up.*

**Q.** Why was the blonde sitting on the roof?

**A.** *Because the drinks are on the house.*

**Q.** What do you call a blonde who doesn't like butter?

**A.** *Marge.*

**Q.** Why does a blonde take the pill?

**A.** *So she knows what day it is.*

**Q.** How do you know if a ransom note has been sent by a blonde?

**A.** *Because it has a stamped, self addressed envelope enclosed.*

**Q.** How do you make a blonde's eyes sparkle?

**A.** *Shine a torch in one ear.*

**Q.** What do you call a blonde who has no arms, no legs and who sits on a pile of leaves?

**A.** *Russell.*

**Q.** How do you know that a blonde has been using your dishwasher?

**A.** *The drain is clogged with the residue of paper plates.*

**Q.** Why do blondes take two hot water bottles to bed?
**A.** *In case one of them leaks.*

**Q.** What is the difference between a blonde and a shopping trolley?
**A.** *A shopping trolley has a mind of its own.*

**Q.** Where would you find a blonde on the day that his ship comes in?
**A.** *At the airport.*

**Q.** What are the best three years of a blonde's life?
**A.** *Year 9 in secondary school.*

**Q.** What is the difference between a ham sandwich and a blonde?
**A.** *A ham sandwich is only five centimetres thick.*

**Q.** What is the difference between 100 ham sandwiches and a blonde?
**A.** *Nothing.*

**Q.** Why do blonde dogs have flat noses?
**A.** *Because they chase parked cars.*

# THEN THERE WAS . . .

**W**omen want a relationship without the complication of unnecessary sex.

Men want sex without the complication of an unnecessary relationship.

**A** blonde was lying in a hospital bed and groaning opened his eyes.

His neighbour, a kindly chap inquired, 'Are you feeling all right?'

'Where am I?'

'Hospital. Do you want the good news or the bad news first?'

'Give me the bad news. I can take it. It can't be any worse than how I feel.'

'Well, you were in a horrible car accident and they have had to cut off both legs.'

'My God, that's awful!'

'Now do you want the good news?'

'You must be joking.'

'No, it's all good, the bloke in the next bed wants to buy your shoes.'

**D**id you hear about the blonde jelly fish?
It set.

**A** brunette explained to the doctor that all her life she wanted to be a blonde.

'Well,' said the doctor, 'There's an operation you can undergo. We just remove a portion of the brain and you will be thinking and talking like a blonde.'

'Right,' said the brunette, 'I'll have it.'

Three weeks later the doctor walked into his patient's room with a very worried expression on his face.

'I've made a terrible mistake,' He explained, 'I've removed 80 per cent of your brain instead of the 20 per cent.'

The blonde grinned, shook the doctor's hand and said, 'She'll be right, mate.'

**A** brunette, a redhead and a blonde were travelling through the desert when their four wheel drive broke down.

They had to walk to the nearest settlement.

'I'll take some water so we won't die of thirst,' said the brunette.

'I'll take some food so that we can restore our energy,' said the redhead.

'I'll take the car door so we can wind down the window when it gets hot,' said the blonde.